Throw Off
What Holds
You Back

Throw *Off*
What Holds
You Back

George Bloomer

Charisma
HOUSE
A STRANG COMPANY

Incidents and persons portrayed in this book are based on fact. Some names, places and any identifying details may have been changed and altered to protect the privacy and anonymity of the individuals to whom they refer. Any similarity between the names and stories of individuals known to readers is coincidental and not intentioned.

Library of Congress Cataloging-in-Publication Data

Bloomer, George G., 1963-
  Throw off what holds you back / George Bloomer.
    p. cm.
  ISBN 1-59185-195-5 (pbk.)
  1. Christian life—Pentecostal authors. I. Title.
  BV4501.3B56 2003
  248.4—dc22

                                2003015022

               03 04 05 06 07 — 87654321
            Printed in the United States of America

To my Advanced Deliverance Team
at Bethel Family Worship Center
and the ministerial staff for their faithful support

To Bishop Eddie L. Long and
Bishop T. D. Jakes
for their creative insight

CONTENTS

Foreword

Are there areas of weakness and turmoil in your life that you don't quite understand? Have you allowed your proclivities, hang-ups, false teachings or traditions to hinder you from reaching your goals and aspirations? Learn how to activate your God-given spiritual authority, and decree and declare that even the demons are subject to you through the name of Christ. When all hell breaks lose, our first inclination as saints of God should not be to flee to a corner and quiver in fear. Rather, we must immediately stand in authority, throw off the spirit of fear and doubt and possess the promises of God.

Luke 10:17 issues a rude awakening to any believer who has ever doubted his or her authority through Christ Jesus:

> Then the seventy returned with joy, saying "Lord, even the demons are subject to us in Your name."

If you have grown tired of the demonic influences of the devil free-loading upon the back of your blessings, then this prolific word of truth is guaranteed to open your eyes and give you the strength to throw off what holds you back and move into the marvelous realm of God's divine blessings.

Bishop Bloomer delivers another blow to the demonic portals of hell as he exposes the spiritual authority that the children of God possess to tread on serpents and scorpions, and over all the power of the enemy. Nothing shall by any means hurt you!

I am constantly amazed at the anointing of God that rests upon the life of Bishop Bloomer. Never before have I met an individual with such spiritual sensitivity to go into the enemy's camp and make a direct hit that sets the captive free without annihilating the community of believers in the process. During his visit to New Birth Missionary Baptist Church, literally hundreds were set free. And they are currently walking in victory, throwing off the demonic influences that held them back and embracing their God-given inheritance.

As an individual who walks in authority, Bishop Bloomer knows firsthand the witchcraft and trickery that the enemy uses to deceive the children of God. After reading this book, you too will know that you no longer have to live a life of mediocrity—compromising your peace and sustaining unnecessary pain. Get ready to be enlightened, delivered and set free from the demonic hindrances of the enemy—and be propelled into a realm of God's truth and blessings.

Throw Off What Holds You Back—your weapon of warfare on how to let go of traditions, attitudes and religious mind-sets. Put off the old man, and be renewed in the spirit of your mind!

—BISHOP EDDIE L. LONG, SENIOR PASTOR
NEW BIRTH MISSIONARY BAPTIST CHURCH
ATLANTA, GEORGIA

Introduction

Throughout my years in ministry, I've come across many great men and women of God who fail to experience their full potential and power in God through Christ Jesus. Why?

The Word of God declares:

> And you shall know the truth, and the truth shall make you free.
>
> —JOHN 8:32

Without truth, there can be no freedom. Hence, many who find shelter beneath the umbrella of ignorance find themselves showered by the abundance of Satan's lies. He tells you who you are, where you're from, where you're going and how you're going to get there. Reside under his lie long enough, and ultimately, his lie becomes your truth.

The truth is that we all have weaknesses, proclivities—thorns in our flesh—with which we struggle on a daily basis. None of these things, however, are a mystery to God:

> O LORD, You have searched me and known me.
> You know my sitting down and my rising up;
> You understand my thought afar off.
> You comprehend my path and my lying down,
> And are acquainted with all my ways.
> For there is not a word on my tongue,
> But behold, O LORD, You know it altogether.
> You have hedged me behind and before,
> And laid Your hand upon me.
>
> —PSALM 139:1–5

God is not intimidated, nor is He shocked, by your present situation. As you continue to seek Him for His guidance, He is committed to seeing you through every secret weakness and every temptation. He is also committed to destroying the curse of the enemy that has been served to you on the illusive platter of Satan's lies.

You must understand the power you possess through Christ Jesus to destroy every curse and to stand boldly "in the liberty by which Christ has made us free" (Gal. 5:1). Regardless of where you come from, the enemy does not have the authority, nor does he have the right, to dictate where you are going. The decision has already been made. Still, the Lord gives you a choice. Life offers many options, both good and bad. It is your decision, however, to determine to choose wisely. The Word tells us, "Enter by the narrow gate; for wide is the gate and broad is the way that leads to destruction, and there are many who go in by it. Because narrow is the gate and difficult is the way which leads to life, and there are few who find it" (Matt. 7:13–14).

> *Regardless of where you come from,*
> *the enemy does not have the authority,*
> *nor does he have the right, to dictate*
> *where you are going.*

If you have made decisions impulsively in the past due to tradition, false religion, anger, fatigue, frustration, lack of faith or even ignorance, now is the time to throw off every myth and lie of the devil and take hold of the promises of God. It's time to throw off what holds you back! My desire has always been, and will remain, that the children of God learn to develop a true and lasting relationship with the Lord Jesus Christ for themselves, sealing the door to false teachings and doctrines of men that come to hinder their walk with God. Many are cursed for heeding the teachings of men over the voice of God, which causes them to spiral into an infinite whirlwind of confusion and deceit. By so doing they begin to question God and His motives when, in fact, it's often their own motives that bring them to their present predicaments in the first place—not the judgment of God.

Now is the time to stop rehearsing all that the enemy has done wrong in your life and to decree that this is a new day and a new time—a day of revelation, a day of change. No longer will you walk by what you see and feel, but you will walk according to the voice of the Lord and His statutes.

Are you aware that self-inflicted curses, or the sins of your forefathers, could be hovering over your life? Have you taken the time to investigate your family history and to renounce those things that your parents and grandparents did that continue to linger in your life today? Now is the time to rid yourself of every accursed thing in your life that has held you back and caused you to lose your focus.

The blessings of God are without discrimination. The way has been paved, and God's blessings sit patiently waiting, readily available to all who will receive God's truth and reject the lies of the devil. If the devil says that you're nothing, know that before you lies greatness. When he torments you with poverty, before you awaits great wealth. When he reminds you of an abusive past, know that God knew you were strong enough to take it, and He wants to use your testimony to rescue someone else. When he reminds you of your mother's or father's rejection, remind him, "When my father and my mother forsake me, then the LORD will take care of me" (Ps. 27:10). When he says you can't do something, tell yourself, "I can do all things through Christ who strengthens me" (Phil. 4:13). Lose every religious lie, renounce every curse, and gain relationship in Jesus Christ.

> Let us lay aside every weight, and the sin which so easily ensnares us, and let us run with endurance the race that is set before us.
>
> —HEBREWS 11:1

Your eyes saw my substance, being yet unformed.
And in Your book they all were written,
The days fashioned for me,
When as yet there were none of them.

———

—PSALM 139:16

One

How Did I Get This Way?

Each of us, based on family history and present environment, develops certain inherent traits and cultural characteristics—some good, some bad. For instance, when researching the history of many great spiritual leaders, behind the scenes you will often find someone who was very instrumental in shaping the spirituality and sense of leadership of that great leader and legend: parents, grandparents, an aunt, an uncle. I'm sure that many of the spiritual values and great leadership abilities of Martin Luther King Sr., which had been developed during his years as pastor of the renowned Ebenezer Baptist Church, spilled over into the life of his son, whom we know today as the great midwife to equality and freedom, Dr. Martin Luther King Jr. The same is true with many successful businesspeople. Success breeds success.

1

A person conforms to the strongest possessing force in his or her environment. Bill Gates's success, for instance, can be traced back to a lineage of strong business-minded men: his father, a prominent lawyer; his grandfather, vice president of a national bank; and his great-grandfather, mayor and state legislator. His success was further attributed to two very keen parents who noticed his intelligence at a young age and enrolled him in a more challenging academic environment, which would serve as the catalyst for him to recognize his destiny, confront opposition and come face-to-face with success.

Sometimes the negative influences of the past can be turned into positive steppingstones to success, as in my own experience. Although my father was not an integral part of my life, leaving more scars and bruises than words of wisdom, the part of him that did everything in a big way rested on my life. It would later prove to be an integral part of my success.

A person conforms to the strongest possessing force in his or her environment.

God knows how to take what the devil meant for bad and transform it to good so that God alone can be glorified in your life. The two driving forces behind my perseverance for a better life were thinking big and refusing to settle for less than what God said I should have. Regardless of how you may feel about your parents, a part of them will always remain inside of you. It's up to you—you must either accept it, try to change it or use it as a steppingstone to propel you to where you need to be.

WHO ARE YOU?

Imagine growing up in a home filled with siblings, each with his or her own distinct, yet similar characteristics, each reflecting the qualities and features of his or her creators—Mom and Dad. You, however, are always on the cutting edge of distinction. People often mistake you for the distant cousin...the nephew...the niece... the neighbor next door. You can't understand why you behave so differently or from where your unique cravings originated. Although you have the routine of the home down to a science and fit perfectly into the puzzle that makes up the family unit, still you remain the unique piece of an unfinished puzzle.

Life goes on as normal, but the constant tug upon the mental chambers of your heart refuses to loosen its grasp. You wonder, *How did I get this way? Why do I feel so different? What is the root cause of this unfulfilled craving and yearning for the unknown?* These questions float within the corridors of your mind, which is searching to unravel the complex mystery. Then one day the truth is revealed: You were adopted. At that moment you realize that you're not delusional or eccentric. Although you were separated at birth from your biological mother and father, that part of you that was extracted from their loins remains as an inescapable memory of God's creative power.

Regardless of your current family situation, you must understand that you are a son or daughter of God. Once you come into the realization of who you are in Christ and that His own hands created you, you receive peace. Doubt is replaced with reassurance, sadness is overcome by joy, timidity is tossed for boldness, and the transformation of the new creation begins. Old things are passed away, and you're entitled to a new beginning.

Having the proper information on where you are from is the most enlightening road map to where you're going. Many of us know what we want to achieve in life. We have goals and aspirations, but many of these dreams fall like dust to the earth because of the hindrances that meet us along the way. Knowing where you're from and why you behave the way you behave shortens the length of the journey, makes the crooked way straight and becomes the light unto your path. Knowing who you are—your weaknesses and your strengths—also gives you a better understanding of the road that you must take to accomplish what can only be done after surrendering to the will of God. Once you say, "Lord, Your will be done in me," the seed that has been lying dormant on the inside finally begins to sprout and take root.

PREGNANT WITH DESTINY

Doctors agree that the most crucial time for an unborn child is the first trimester of the mother's pregnancy. Her habits, her emotions and what she consumes are all crucial elements in the full development of the child. A healthy environment plays a crucial part in stimulating proper growth. The mother's appetite is no longer her own. Instead, it is steered, stimulated and ruled by the miracle of life that is growing within.

The same is true when you, as a believer in Christ, come into the full knowledge of Christ Jesus and the powerful seed of life you carry within. Your appetite is no longer your own. Your earnest prayer becomes, "Not my will, Lord, but Your will be done." Just as the pregnant mother experiences discomfort, fatigue, mood swings and stress in the natural, you will experience the same things in the Spirit. You may not always understand the feelings you have or your mood swings, but you can trust God to do whatever it takes to insure a healthy delivery. Your discomfort is only for a season, and your appetite is no longer being steered by your own desires. It is being guided by the destiny you are about to birth from within.

> *Having the proper information*
> *on where you are from is the most*
> *enlightening road map to*
> *where you're going.*

As an expectant mother completes her first trimester and eases her way into the second, she finds that the adjustment becomes much easier to bear. The things that bothered her in the first trimester will most likely disappear in the second. She can hear the baby's heartbeat and see his development. You too will find that as long as you don't give up during the initial stages of your spiritual pregnancy, reaching your destiny will no longer seem like a nagging discomfort or unreachable dream. Soon you will hear the spiritual heartbeat of your destiny, and you will feel it stretching its limbs.

A living, breathing miracle is growing on the inside, just waiting for the right time to reveal itself to the world. As it grows, you grow along with it. You can see it coming into fruition, and you will embrace each new stage of spiritual growth with expectancy. Your testimony becomes, "Come what may, I must give birth to this seed that's going to change my life forever!"

Finally, it's time to give birth. The pain seems unbearable for some mothers, and they will require medication to ease the discomfort and to concentrate on the birth. Pushing at the right time, not panicking and following the instructions of the doctor are extremely important during the birthing process.

The same is true with your spiritual seed. That is why it is so important for you to be under good spiritual leadership while you are pregnant with destiny. The right leader will see what lies within your womb, prevent you from pushing too soon and teach you how to stay calm during seasons of pain. Sometimes the pain is so unbearable that the natural inclination to push before your time causes you to jeopardize the safety of your seed. Nevertheless, your spiritual doctor, Dr. Jesus, knows how to guide you safely through the delivery of your spiritual destiny. You need only to trust and obey His commands.

GIVING GOD DIRECTIONS

A problem arises, however, when a person who has cried out to God with the needs within his heart begins to tell God how to answer those needs. "Dear God, I want to be successful in life. I want to know You, Lord, and to gain a closer walk with You. *But God, please don't let me suffer in any way.*" With success and growth comes sacrifice. Although *suffering* can be a very intimidating word, as children of God, it's often a very necessary component of spiritual growth:

> And if children, then heirs—heirs of God and joint
> heirs with Christ, if indeed we suffer with Him,
> that we may also be glorified together. For I con-
> sider that the sufferings of this present time are
> not worthy to be compared with the glory which
> shall be revealed in us.
>
> —ROMANS 8:17–18

The question then becomes, "How much are you willing to give up in order to gain all that you need?" As a little boy growing up in the projects of Brooklyn, New York, I always knew that I wanted to be someone "important." I wanted the big, shiny, mahogany desk, complete with the big chair and cozy office. The initial fulfillment of this dream came by way of an old discarded desk and chair that I retrieved from the garbage and managed to drag to the bedroom of the apartment complex in Red Hook Projects where my family lived. I was nine years old and CEO of a "no-name" company that was very real to me. It was all completely funded and operated by the dreams of a young boy whom God allowed to glimpse into the future and take a quick peek at destiny.

I was also inspired by great men of God who had such an amazing handle on the Word of God that they had the faith and audacity to call upon God to do things that others only imagined could unfold upon the big screen of one of Hollywood's finest flicks. I developed great respect and adoration for their ability to possess so much power while remaining humble enough to reach each person at his or her own level of under-standing. "God, I want to be a great man of God!" was often my inner cry.

God answered by allowing me to go through abuse, rejection, bad relationships, drug addiction, incarceration, and marital and emotional trials. Today I am able to minister to a multifaceted number of people, each at his or her own level of understanding and life experience.

> *Your present environment does not have to dictate to you your final destination.*

Not every person's success is birthed out of this level of trauma and suffering, but this is the path that was necessary for me in order to become the man that God had ordained me to be. Had I not gone through those things, I would not be able to impact effectively the lives of countless people with whom I come into contact daily, who want to know one thing: "Bishop, how can I make my life better and once and for all be set free?" Through my testimony, people are introduced to a God who is real, attainable and effective. Today, as a successful man with a not-so-successful past, I'm able to teach others the way to success, how to keep it and the meaning of true wealth.

A MIND TO SUCCEED

Success is a mind-set. It doesn't come once you have the material wealth to prove it, but it shines through your actions, the way you think, how you behave and how you prioritize your life. The writer of Proverbs teaches valuable principles for keeping your focus in spite of your present environment:

When you sit down to eat with a ruler,
Consider carefully what is before you;
And put a knife to your throat
If you are a man given to appetite.
Do not desire his delicacies,
For they are deceptive food.

Do not overwork to be rich;
Because of your own understanding, cease!
Will you set your eyes on that which is not?
For riches certainly make themselves wings;
They fly away like an eagle toward heaven.

Do not eat the bread of a miser,
Nor desire his delicacies;
For as he thinks in his heart, so is he.
"Eat and drink!" he says to you,
But his heart is not with you.
The morsel you have eaten, you will vomit up,
And waste your pleasant words.

—PROVERBS 23:1–8

I've found that my greatest wealth is not in material gain, but it is reflected in those whose lives the Lord has allowed me to touch and to speak into as I hear His voice and obey His command.

Now that you know where you're from, decide where you're going and how much you're willing to give in order to get there. Your present environment does not have to dictate to you your final destination. God's desire for you is clear. He says in Deuteronomy 30:19, "I have set before you life and death, blessing and cursing; therefore choose life, that both you and your descendants may live."

What does this mean? Simply stated, it means that we have a choice.

It is the Lord's will that you abide in the bountiful blessings of life. But He will not override your desire to remain under the oppressive curse of degradation, poverty, sin and disbelief. Along with the measure of faith that He has issued to you, however, He has also provided instructions on how to turn your oppressive state into steppingstones that lift you to victory, eternally abandoning your valley of defeat.

As a young boy growing up in the welfare system, I witnessed firsthand the dependency and complacency that can develop when dreams are lost and where each hurdle seems to become nothing more than agony and continual defeat. As I witnessed my family's dependency on government assistance, this same dependency began to spill over into my adult life. Rather than seek God for my daily sufficiency, I began thinking that people should automatically give to me and accommodate me when needed.

Today, as it is with many impoverished urban cultures, poverty and hopelessness can become the norm, while peace of mind, success and the ability to dream become unrealistic expectations associated with those who are out of touch with reality. But although your environment may try to bully you against a wall of defeat, never cease to keep your eyes on the prize, which is your dreams and visions. This will give you the strength you need to persevere, to aim high and to claim the victory.

THE CURSE OF COMPLACENCY

The most priceless commodity is the mind, but if it has been tainted and brainwashed with delusions of defeat, it will inevitably become a minefield of dreams deferred, disappointments and unrealized potential. Those who dare to think big often run headfirst into a wall of controversy, built by others whose minds are victims of what I call *the curse of complacency.*

Unlike pure satisfaction, complacency says, "This is the state that I'm in. I don't like it, but this is where I'm going to remain; it's more comfortable for me here." Complacency builds a community of self-satisfaction with a welcome sign that reads, "This is the town that fear built."

It is always better to challenge the disappointments and claim the victory rather than bow down and remain a slave. The thought of illuminating those dark, unsuccessful areas in the community of self-satisfaction with success often seems too far-fetched or unimaginable. Either the mere thought of failure is too much to bear, or the reality of success is too thought provoking—too good to be true.

Always remember that if you're ever going to be a great success, you must make some failures first. What if when a baby took his first step and fell down, he became so frustrated and stubborn that he refused to take another step ever again? His limbs would plead with him to try again, but his fear of failure would grip his growth and limit his future. Consider your current environment as merely a starting point. Where you wind up and how fast you get there hinge upon the decisions you make and how passionate you are about getting there. Regardless of what you have gone through, you cannot allow the stigma and trauma to prolong the generational curses that have been hovering over your life, nor can you allow them to stunt your growth.

GENERATIONAL CURSES

Generational curses are exactly what their name implies—curses passed down from generation to generation. Whether it's through illnesses, such as heart disease or depression, or the result of other problems, generational curses are very real. Doctors will agree that certain health risks are passed down from generation to generation. It is for that reason that often much of the time you spend during a visit to the doctor may be revisiting the past—outlining not only your medical history, but also the medical history of your parents and grandparents.

> *Where you wind up and how fast you get there hinge upon the decisions you make and how passionate you are about getting there.*

Christians should be aware of generational curses and how they affect their families. We must be proactive in renouncing them and preventing the cycle of recurring illnesses, mental and emotional breakdowns, divorces, drug addictions and other problems related to family history.

It is a misconception that Christians cannot be cursed. This teaching prevents those who are living under a curse from being set free. If a new convert is led to believe that he cannot be cursed, he will dismiss the possibility of an unknown curse that might be at work in his life, explaining away the problem as something else. This spiritual misdiagnosis causes him to live in a state of repression rather than experiencing the power of confession, which ultimately sets the captive free.

In this book we will take an in-depth look at the effects of curses, their origins and how to break them. For instance, did you realize that the family often pays the price for the sins of the parents and the grandparents? The sins you commit today will ultimately affect your children of tomorrow. This topic is often overlooked and seldom taught, but it remains a nagging problem with which the children of God struggle continually.

As you read, you may be shocked to discover that many of the spiritual principles and traditional teachings you were taught have been your greatest hindrances. It is my prayer that this book will serve as your wake-up call to deliverance.

Beware lest any man spoil you through philosophy and vain deceit, after the tradition of men, after the rudiments of the world, and not after Christ.

———————

—COLOSSIANS 2:8, KJV

Two

Deliverance From Trashy Traditions

Imagine a seventeen-year-old girl who, despite her youth and inexperience, has just given birth to a healthy and happy baby. She's thrilled that the worst is finally over. The morning sickness, aches, pain and fear of the unknown are a memory of the gift, the reward for bearing all of the necessary pain. She realizes that she can't change the past, but she's finally ready to move on and face her future. As maternal instincts begin to materialize, she curls up with her miraculous bundle of joy, takes a deep breath and nurtures this gift of life.

Suddenly she hears the urgent knocking of bad news pounding on her front door. It's the authorities. They have come to inform the young mother that on the following morning she will be punished. No, she hasn't robbed, killed, stolen anything or even lied to anyone. Rather, according to Islamic law, she has committed

15

the sin of having a child out of wedlock. Although she's endured nine months of emotional and physical transformation, she now discovers that the real mental and emotional anguish are just about to begin.

Believe it or not, this is the true story of a young Nigerian girl by the name of Bariya Ibrahim Magazu, who was sentenced to a public whipping of 180 lashes with a cane for bearing a child out of wedlock. The world was not only amazed but also shocked at the audacity of her accusers and the severity of the punishment invoked on this young girl, all in the name of Islamic religion and tradition.[1]

Upon hearing this story, I'm sure you gasped in utter disbelief at the cruelty of such a punishment on anyone, much less a frightened young girl who has just given birth and is still breast-feeding her newly arrived infant. Yet, many women in our Christian churches continue to bear the brunt of attack from accusers who sentence them according to their "crimes of passion." And although their spiritual floggings don't leave physical scars, the damage done to their mental and emotional state of mind can be just as treacherous.

I remember growing up in the church amidst strict rules of conduct and unwritten laws of discipline for women who were "caught" in sin. A woman, for instance, who became pregnant out of wedlock was made to be a public example by those who intended to preserve the façade of a sin-free church. Regardless of what her duties in the church had been—whether ushering, singing in the choir or greeting at the door—she was forced to relinquish those duties and take a seat in the back of the church until her accusers found her "worthy" of resuming her position. Some traditions, including the disciplining of women for their sins while their male counterparts are protected from such public humiliation, are practices deeply embedded within the history of religion.

CONDEMNATION

In the eighth chapter of John, Jesus demonstrated His heart of compassion in the midst of a community's condemnation toward just such a woman. Early one morning as He was teaching in the temple, He was confronted by an angry group of scribes and Pharisees who brought to Him a woman they had caught in the act of adultery. "Teacher, this woman was caught in adultery, in the very act," they told him (John 8:4). Then they continued, reciting to Him the traditional response they had been taught to make in such a situation: "Now Moses, in the law, commanded us that such should be stoned" (v. 5).

> ### Christ has already made it clear
> ### that His purpose is not to condemn.

These scribes and Pharisees were merely looking for a reason to accuse Jesus of not abiding by the traditions of their Jewish religion. But Jesus was not bound by religious tradition, and He responded not with condemnation, but with compassion:

> But Jesus stooped down and wrote on the ground with His finger, as though He did not hear. So when they continued asking Him, He raised Himself up and said to them, "He who is without

sin among you, let him throw a stone at her first."
And again He stooped down and wrote on the
ground.

Then those who heard it, being convicted by
their conscience, went out one by one, beginning
with the oldest even to the last. And Jesus was left
alone, and the woman standing in the midst.
When Jesus had raised Himself up and saw no
one but the woman, He said to her, "Woman,
where are those accusers of yours? Has no man
condemned you?"

She said, "No one, Lord."

And Jesus said to her, "Neither do I condemn
you; go and sin no more."

—JOHN 8:6–11

If Jesus has enough restraint not to condemn but to
allow His compassion to flush away sin, then who are
we to invoke such harsh, unjustifiable punishments on
those who have made wrong decisions? John 3:17 says,
"For God did not send His Son into the world to
condemn the world, but that the world through Him
might be saved."

When you find someone condemning an individual,
supposedly for "the sake of Christ," be aware that
Christ has nothing to do with it. He has already made it
clear that His purpose is not to condemn. Who are we
to take matters into our own hands? Yet, that is exactly
what is taking place when a person is being emotionally
and spiritually stoned to death and we do nothing
about it. Instead, we become like the crowd in Jesus'
day, standing by idly, watching the accusers of the

woman lash out at her, while many of them were guilty of the same thing.

The scribes and Pharisees who were accusing Jesus were not only trying to use law and tradition to accuse the woman—they were intent on ensnaring Jesus with it also. But Jesus is too wise for such entrapment. He remembers that we all have sinned—a fact that mankind often forgets.

This does not excuse acts of immorality and sin. But as believers, we must never forget that it is God who makes the final sentence on a person's life—not mankind. Just because the sins of some become public, while others remain covert acts of immorality, does not make one sin greater than another. Be careful of those who are quick to bring the sins of individuals to light while dimming the lights on their own shortcomings. None of the men gathered in the crowd around Jesus that day were willing to take Him up on His ultimatum of casting the first stone. This indicated that none of the men were without sin. They chose to flee rather than risk the inevitable unveiling of their own shortcomings and scandals.

FAIR JUDGMENT

> Judge not, that you be not judged. For with what judgment you judge, you will be judged; and with the measure you use, it will be measured back to you. And why do you look at the speck in your brother's eye, but do not consider the plank in your own eye?
> —MATTHEW 7:1–3

The true message in this scripture is not that we shouldn't judge at all, but simply that when our shortcomings come to light, we will be judged based upon how we have judged others in the past. Sometimes we can become so blinded by the ritualistic method of doing things that we fail to judge each case individually and fairly with godly intentions. When we do this, our motives are impure, and we overlook the root cause of the sin and the need to get people set free.

Although all traditions are not bad, even the good ones can be abused by those who seek blood from the enemy's already wounded prey. Such people use tradition simply as an excuse to inflict further pain. Some traditions were created with the best intentions at heart, yet often they cause more harm than good. This dilemma leaves one to wonder, *Is preserving tradition even worth it?*

A classic example occurs during the holiday season when families are supposed to come together for a joyous occasion of family fellowship. But what if the family is not joyous and all they do is fuss and fight? Family members cannot sit in a room together for more than five minutes without a barroom brawl breaking out. Everyone goes home feeling miserable, but they meet again the following year to do it all over again. Why? Because tradition says that families are supposed to be together during the holidays. But at what cost, and what if it's not working?

Why not come up with a different plan for unifying the family rather than subjecting everyone to miserable memories year after year?

Gauging yourself by the Word of God, how many of your personal traditions have been making the people around you miserable? Believe it or not, even your religion can become a stumbling block if it's presented

to a nonbeliever in a self-righteous
vents that person from seeing the love of

EATING WITH DIRTY HANDS

Traditions are built on past rituals, which conti
from generation to generation. They develop mind-sets
that can sometimes become so strong that not even
truth can penetrate the false perception of life. When
Jesus refers to traditions in the Bible, it's normally in the
form of a rebuke. That's because many traditions produce a stubborn mind-set that is stronger than a
person's ability to receive the Word of God and be set
free. Many times even in church we place traditional
value above our purpose—which is to meet the need of
the people, introduce them to the person of Jesus
Christ and get them set free.

Having a self-righteous mind-set can dim the light to
your own flaws while illuminating the weaknesses of
others. In Mark 7, the Pharisees were very quick to
point out the "audacity" of the disciples to eat bread
with "unwashed hands," a blatant disrespect to the tradition of the elders:

> Then the Pharisees and some of the scribes came
> together to Him, having come from Jerusalem.
> Now when they saw some of His disciples eat
> bread with defiled, that is, with unwashed, hands,
> they found fault. For the Pharisees and all the
> Jews do not eat unless they wash their hands in a
> special way, holding the tradition of the elders.
> When they come from the marketplace, they do
> not eat unless they wash. And there are many

eceived and hold,

ers, copper vessels,

risees and scribes

disciples not walk

f the elders, but eat

"

—Mᴀʀᴋ 7:1–5

arisees were just trying to
ontraditional" conduct of
His disciples, and He responded with a rebuke to the
Pharisees. "How dare you place your tradition above
the teachings of the Word of God, and then judge the
disciples for eating without washing their hands?" Like
the crowd gathered around the woman brought to
Jesus in adultery, the Pharisees were complaining about
the dirty hands of Jesus' disciples when their own hands
were spiritually filthy.

The Pharisees were prepared to invoke harsh punishment on the disciples for disobeying tradition, but Jesus
pointed out their own hypocrisies. He rebuked them
for "laying aside the commandment of God" in order to
keep their own traditions.

> He answered and said to them, "Well did Isaiah
> prophesy of you hypocrites, as it is written: 'This
> people honors Me with their lips, but their heart
> is far from Me. And in vain they worship Me,
> teaching as doctrines the commandments of
> men.' For laying aside the commandment of
> God, you hold the tradition of men—the washing
> of pitchers and cups, and many other such things
> you do." He said to them, "All too well you reject

> the commandment of God, that you may keep
> your tradition…making the word of God of no
> effect through your tradition."
>
> —Mark 7:6–9, 13

The power of tradition should never be stronger than the power of God residing inside of us, which enables us to do *His* will above the will of our flesh. What if the government passed a law stating that everyone had to bow down to other gods during certain times of the year, despite religious beliefs? Many would be appalled, protests would break out, and the Christian church would be in an uproar.

BOW DOWN AND WORSHIP

It doesn't take very long for the traditions of men to masquerade as religious piety and devotion. Do you remember how the children of Israel introduced a golden calf into their worship experience? (See Exodus 32.) Unwilling to wait patiently for Moses to return from meeting with God on the mountain, Aaron led the people of God to devise a new tradition—substituting man's god for an encounter with the one true God. Since that moment, at times the people of God have substituted their traditions, their "gods," for a life-transforming encounter with God.

In our world today we see how men's traditions have become religious rituals that are substituting for a relationship with our Lord and Savior Jesus Christ. Many Christians who would never accept a government-mandated law to bow down to other gods have no problem attending ceremonies and vigils where the name of Jesus Christ is not allowed. Most of us see our attendance at such events as an innocent way for people to come together as one. Yet it is similar to what Nebuchadnezzar did when he commanded the people to worship the image. Like Nebuchadnezzar's subjects, we are once again being asked to worship a substitute god.

> Nebuchadnezzar the king made an image of gold, whose height was sixty cubits and its width six cubits. He set it up in the plain of Dura, in the province of Babylon...Then a herald cried aloud, "To you it is commanded, O peoples, nations, and languages, that at the time you hear the sound of the horn, flute, harp, lyre, and psaltery, in symphony with all kinds of music, you shall fall down and worship the gold image that King Nebuchadnezzar has set up; and whoever does not fall down and worship shall be cast immediately into the midst of a burning fiery furnace."
> —DANIEL 3:1, 4–6

Most Christian denominations agree on two things:

1. The Bible is the authentic Word of God to His people.

2. The only way to God is through Jesus Christ.

These two things are the foundation stones to our faith and the steppingstones to a life-changing relationship with God. But because of the traditions of men that have been elevated to expressions of religious performance, many believers have developed mind-sets that open them to receive the teachings of false doctrines.

There is no doubt about it—when you stand up for what you believe, you will always come under fire. When the fire hits, the challenge becomes:

- Are you willing to risk being thrown into the mental and emotional fiery furnace of your accusers?

- Or will you bow down in order to save your life?

> For whoever desires to save his life will lose it, but whoever loses his life for My sake will find it. For what profit is it to a man if he gains the whole world, and loses his own soul? Or what will a man give in exchange for his soul?
>
> —MATTHEW 16:25–26

Ask yourself this: "Is my soul for sale? If so, for how much?" Although this may sound like an appalling question, the truth of the matter is that every time you compromise the teachings of the Word of God for society's tradition, you place a price tag on the Word of God, which resides inside of you.

There is no doubt about it—when you stand up for what you believe, you will always come under fire.

You must maintain the mind of Christ to prevent yourself from giving in to the unreasonable demands of the masses. To maintain the mind of Christ, you might first need to be introduced to Him as a living, breathing part of your existence. This may require change in your mind-set and way of thinking, especially if everything you have ever learned about the Lord was in the form of some cute Sunday school Bible story, which often fictionalizes the name and the Person of Christ.

The Scriptures are not old wives' fables; the Bible is the living Word of God left as factual instructions on how to bind every curse and release the blessings of God over your life. You must have a revelation of how applying the Word of God daily can change your mind and life. Only then will you truly know the Man whom many of us refer to intimately as "Father" and "Lord." His name is *Jesus,* and to truly know Him is to have a divine encounter and truly personal relationship with Him.

MORONIC MIND-SETS

A *mind-set* is having a mind that is set on a particular way of thinking, which is shaped by environmental surroundings and embedded with the powerful influence of good and bad teachings. Moronic mind-sets are minds that have been so contaminated with false teachings that they have been rendered incapable of receiving the truth.

Every parent understands the power of persuasion and the responsibility that each of us has to properly steer a child toward a well-balanced way of thinking. As a pastor, I often counsel individuals whose minds have developed a moronic mind-set that—unless the Lord intervenes—renders them powerless from receiving proper guidance. They wander aimlessly within a miserable box with no exits and no way of escape, the result of bad teaching, a bad upbringing or bad influences. For proper deliverance to take place, order must be set and a sound plan of evacuation executed to lead those who have become comfortable in their bondage to freedom.

Moses learned a great deal from the Israelites concerning disorder and its ability to keep the children of God in bondage. They were so engulfed in their own traditions and mind-sets that even when truth stared them in the face, they remained incapable of seeing it.

THE LAND OF MILK AND HONEY

> Then the LORD said to Moses, "Depart and go up from here, you and the people whom you have brought out of the land of Egypt, to the land of which I swore to Abraham, Isaac, and Jacob, saying, 'To your descendants I will give it.' And I will send My Angel before you, and I will drive out the Canaanite and the Amorite and the Hittite and the Perizzite and the Hivite and the Jebusite. Go up to a land flowing with milk and honey."
>
> —EXODUS 33:1–3

When the Old Testament refers to "the land flowing with milk and honey," we often speak of a prosperous land overflowing with all of our daily necessities. Many of our modern-day spiritual lands of "milk and honey," however, refer to disorderly lifestyles where the crops are overgrown due to overfertilization and giants who inhabit our promised land.

In Exodus 3:8, the Lord made a promise to the children of Israel: "So I have come down to deliver them out of the hand of the Egyptians, and to bring them up from that land to a good and large land, to a land flowing with milk and honey." When they got there, however, their blessing of milk and honey was over-shadowed by the giants that inhabited the land.

What are the giants that are currently squatting on your land of promise and overshadowing the blessings and promises of God in your life? In Numbers 13:28, the giants of the land referred to the descendents of Anak—known hirelings who disrupt and cause chaos in the lives of the children of God. Before the children of Israel could lay claim to their promise, they had to bring order to the Promised Land.

> Now the LORD spoke to Moses in the plains of Moab by the Jordan, across from Jericho, saying, "Speak to the children of Israel, and say to them: 'When you have crossed the Jordan into the land of Canaan, then you shall drive out all the inhabitants of the land from before you, destroy all their engraved stones, destroy all their molded images, and demolish all their high places; you shall dispossess the inhabitants of the land and dwell in it, for I have given you the land to possess.'"
> —NUMBERS 33:50–53

Indeed, the Lord had already given the children of Israel the land, but He caused them to get rid of every trace of ungodly tradition and religion before inhabiting their land flowing with milk and honey.

God told Moses that He was going to bring the children of Israel into a land that was sworn to their forefathers—to Abraham, Isaac and Jacob. He warned, however, that He could not bring the children of Israel out of Egypt until they learned the lessons of Egypt.

When the children of Israel came out of Egypt, they

were exceedingly rich because they had learned the trades of the world while they were in the world. They were later able to implement the training that they had learned through the worldly Egyptian system within the church. So God took them from an ungodly order and establishment to a godly establishment. Yet, when they arrived there, they were afraid. They were afraid because of the reports of giants in the land.

Before the children of Israel had even taken a glimpse of their land of promise, they complained continually about the routes they had to take to get there and the trials they had experienced along the way. This angered God, and if Moses had not interceded on their behalf, they would have wandered on the way without the presence of the Lord:

> "... for I will not go up in your midst, lest I consume you on the way, for you are a stiff-necked people." And when the people heard this bad news, they mourned, and no one put on his ornaments. For the LORD had said to Moses, "Say to the children of Israel, 'You are a stiff-necked people. I could come up into your midst in one moment and consume you. Now therefore, take off your ornaments, that I may know what to do to you.'" So the children of Israel stripped themselves of their ornaments by Mount Horeb.
>
> —EXODUS 33:3–6

What giant is occupying your land of promise? Be careful not to complain while being delivered from your bondage. Although you may feel some discomfort along the way, remember what God has promised to you as your final destination. It's not the trials that you experience along the way that will destroy you. The way you react in the midst of the trials, and the lessons you learn or fail to learn, will ultimately determine whether or not you enjoy the fruits of your promised land. God is about to bring order to what He has already anointed you to do, but first He must strip you of some things so that you may be properly adorned to fill your position in the kingdom.

Regardless of what you have been gifted to do, if you don't have order, that gift or talent will do more harm to you than good. God wants to place you in a position of trust—where you can hear His voice and obey His command without question. Often we cannot hear the voice of God because the traditions we've been taught and our past environments speak louder than His truth.

> *The way you react in the midst of the*
> *trials will ultimately determine*
> *whether or not you enjoy the fruits*
> *of your promised land.*

Until you can impose certain disciplines upon yourself without the whip of man conducting your show and steering your destiny, you will never come into the full manifestation of the plan of God for your life. Leaders represent the voice of God that leads you to the Source. But for complete order to come into your life, you must take the initiative to bring order to your life before crossing over into the fulfillment of true success.

It may seem that the Lord has given you a hard thing to do, but whatever He requires will be a necessary component for your future holistic success and well-being. He may require that you make some drastic changes in your life—such as loosing some ungodly ties. You may even be placed into a season of boredom, where there's nothing you can do except seek the face of God.

THE BLESSING OF BOREDOM

> Then Moses said to the LORD, "See, You say to me, 'Bring up this people.' But You have not let me know whom You will send with me. Yet You have said, 'I know you by name, and you have also found grace in My sight.' Now therefore, I pray, if I have found grace in Your sight, show me now Your way, that I may know You and that I may find grace in Your sight. And consider that this nation is Your people." And He said, "My Presence will go with you, and I will give you rest."
> —EXODUS 33:12–14

When Moses had this conversation with God, he had just come down from the mountain of God to discover that the Israelites had grown impatient waiting for God and had created a golden calf to worship. Their disobedience had so angered God that He said, "Go up...for I will not go up in your midst, lest I consume you on the way, for you are a stiff-necked people" (Exod. 33:3).

So Moses finds himself left alone by God...well, not quite alone. He was standing in the midst of a couple million disobedient Israelites whom he was trying to lead out of bondage. No wonder he said, "You say You aren't going with us, so whom are You going to send with me?"

When Moses left Egypt to lead the Israelites to the

Promised Land, he had been given a clear mandate from God: "Come now, therefore, and I will send you to Pharaoh that you may bring My people, the children of Israel, out of Egypt...I will bring you up out of the affliction of Egypt...to a land flowing with milk and honey" (Exod. 3:10, 17). But now, stuck in the wilderness with disobedient people, alone, because God said He would no longer accompany them, his mission no longer seemed very clear. His faith in God's plan had given way to frustration and failure.

You can't allow people to frustrate the purpose of God in your life. When frustration sets in, it is crucial to find out right away what God is commanding you to do in order to possess your moment of destiny. The disobedience of the children of Israel ushered them—and Moses—into a wilderness experience of spiritual death.

Perhaps there are some things in your life that must die spiritually before the Lord's presence can go with you to your land of promise. Never before has it become more pertinent to reject everything that has hindered you or caused you to miss God and your moment of truth. Cast off the traditions of man, and wait patiently for the Lord to be your helper.

Moses asked God for a helper to "show me now Your way, that I may know You and that I may find grace in Your sight." God replied, "My Presence will go with you, and I will give you rest" (Exod. 33:13–14).

Moses was to rely solely upon the eyes of God and the plan of God. Though the way of the Lord may often appear obstructed by life's challenging hurdles, He reminds us in Isaiah 55:8, "'For My thoughts are not your thoughts, nor are your ways My ways,' says the LORD."

This was not the first opportunity Moses had experienced when he learned the lesson of relying on God alone. In Exodus 24 we see that God prepared Moses for the time when he would be led by God through years of wandering aimlessly on the backside of the mountain through the wilderness.

In that earlier experience, God placed Moses on the backside of the mountain in order to teach him and train him. Moses stayed on the backside of the mountain for forty years. His assignment was so delicate and decisive that God didn't want the intrusion of other voices to persuade Moses' decisions and interrupt the voice of God. God knew that in order for Moses to be effective, he had to know without a doubt when the Lord was speaking and not hesitate in moving on His instructions.

For years prior to that experience, Moses had been surrounded by a multitude of crowds. God wanted Moses to gain a great appreciation for boredom in order to gain a greater appreciation for the presence of God.

The problem that hinders many of us from hearing the voice of God is the intrusion of all of the other voices to whom we're so quick to run instead of seeking God first. Though it can often be an uncomfortable state to be in, boredom is often a great blessing. It forces us to call upon God and seek Him when no one else is there to bail us out. If you don't gain a great appreciation for boredom now, then when you become successful you will begin to gauge your success and happiness based upon things "happening" around you. If nothing "significant" is happening in your life, or if no one is around, you'll begin searching—most likely in all the wrong places—for fulfillment and temporal satisfaction when

God could be trying to use that time to speak to you. Sometimes God just wants to take you to a place of rest where your inner being can communicate with the outer being. It is at that state where your inner conscience begins to speak loudly, rehearsing both the good and bad, weighing your options and ultimately leading you to seek God for the right decisions and give Him the praise for His awesome and mighty works.

God is the only one in the universe who has ever had to be all by Himself—completely alone. How did God do it before the eternities ever came into existence? There were no trees, no wind, no sound, no thunder, no utterances—just God alone. And when God was finished with being by Himself, He said, "I feel like revealing Myself to something." In order to do that He had to create something, so He created grass and greenery of the earth, trees, cattle and birds. As He perused the great vastness of His awesome creations, perhaps then He decided, "Though all of these things are wonderful, they're not giving me the praise that I desire." In His divine sovereignty, He created man, blew into his nostrils the breath of life, and man became a living soul who looked up, beheld God in His glory and testified, "I love You, Lord." Immediately God knew that He had found what He had been looking for. Remember that God wants what comes out of Him to give praise back to Him.

When God placed Moses on the backside of the mountain, Moses was able to get a serious picture of God, His nature and His character. Moses discovered that all the time he spent alone, he really wasn't alone at all. He was spending time with God. But spending time with God also disfellowshiped Moses from mankind. So there was a part of Moses that didn't know how to deal with people because he had been with God so long. He forgot that his displeasure for sin and his ability to do without fleshly desires far exceeded the discipline of men who had already grown weary of their discomfort and begun to call upon other "gods" to fill the void.

The reason some individuals can't deal with people is because they're so "deep" and have been with God so long that they can't communicate with people here on earth. So Moses, who had the insight and the mandate, was looking for someone to communicate with the people.

No one told Moses to go up the mountain after the children of God had crossed the Red Sea, but it was Moses' character that forced him to that private place. When leadership was demanded from Moses and he needed to be able to convey his thoughts and values to mankind, he was unable to do it. Although Moses had fallen into sin earlier, he now hated it and detached himself from it. He had forgotten where he had come from, and people had begun to get on his nerves. Now that he had moved out of the season of striking rocks and into the season of speaking the Word to fulfill God's purpose, he let people force him back into striking. Moses had finally gotten the children of Israel out of Egypt; yet, they wound up spending forty years in the wilderness due to their disobedience, which invoked a self-inflicted curse.

Can you imagine how Moses may have felt after basking in the presence of the Lord for forty days and nights? After he had communed with God and received divine instructions to propel the children of Israel into their next level of divine fulfillment, the Lord commanded him:

> Go, get down! For your people whom you have brought out of the land of Egypt have corrupted themselves.
>
> —EXODUS 32:7

As Moses journeyed out of the mount, his ears were tuned to a troubling sound. The sound of music, dancing and shouting resonated throughout the atmosphere of the camp.

> Now when the children of Israel saw that Moses delayed coming down from the mountain, the people gathered together to Aaron, and said to him, "Come, make us gods that shall go before us."
>
> —EXODUS 32:1

The outcome of their request was a golden calf, which they worshiped in the place of God. Dishonoring their covenant to the Lord, they corrupted themselves with idolatry. Amazed and heartbroken by what he saw as he came down the mount, Moses became outraged.

> So it was, as soon as he came near the camp, that he saw the calf and the dancing. So Moses' anger became hot, and he cast the tablets out of his hands and broke them at the foot of the mountain.
>
> —EXODUS 32:19

Because he had spent time with God, Moses had a divine revelation of the precious gifts that the children of Israel were jeopardizing–their lives, their destiny and their relationship with God. Their impatience had caused them to take matters into their own hands and worship a false god rather than take time to receive revelation from the true and living God regarding their lives and their futures.

LESSONS IN BONDAGE

Regardless of what your experiences are, if you don't have a revelation beyond your experience, you're going to die at the end of your experience. How traumatic it must be for your leader to die before he or she has had a chance to impart into you, or before giving you the key to unlock the door. Moses would never enter the Promised Land. All he could do was look at the land from the top of a mountain while still on the wilderness side of freedom.

When you long for the trashy traditions of old, you curse yourself and hinder the blessings of God.

God called Moses to the top of Mount Pisgah. "And the LORD showed him all the land ... Then the LORD said to him ... 'I have caused you to see it with your eyes, but you shall not cross over there'" (Deut. 34:1, 4). What God was saying to Moses is, "The mountain you once stood behind is the mountain you are now going to stand upon. You have to get behind it before you can stand on it. You must stoop before you conquer and sacrifice before you reign. In order to have a great standing, you may have to go under first."

By spending time in the wilderness, Moses had conquered the tradition of being driven by events. He had gained a great appreciation for boredom. If you want to be successful, sometimes you must be willing to break out of the box and ask the Lord to give you something that you can understand.

God allows you to go through what you go through so that He can reveal Himself to you and show you things about yourself. God can't reveal Himself to you when you are so caught up in yourself. When the children of Israel complained incessantly to Moses, he "cried out to the LORD, saying, 'What shall I do with this people?'" (Exod. 17:4). He was engaged in serious warfare, but he knew that he must let God give him the solution to his problem. Be willing to cry out to God by saying, "What shall I do?" Too many times we ask God to deliver us from the devil's snare when the devil has nothing to do with our present situation. Be aware that God might be using the pressure you feel to make you into the person He wants you to be. Determine at the onset that you will not crack under the pressure.

What have you learned from your bondage? Is the road to freedom so bumpy that you are trying to turn around and return to slavery? After receiving the report of giants in the land, the children of Israel began to grumble, complain and long for their bondage:

> So all the congregation lifted up their voices and cried, and the people wept that night. And all the children of Israel complained against Moses and Aaron, and the whole congregation said to them, "If only we had died in the land of Egypt! Or if only we had died in this wilderness! Why has the LORD brought us to this land to fall by the sword, that our

wives and children should become victims? Would
it not be better for us to return to Egypt?"
—NUMBERS 14:1–4

Can you imagine being led out of bondage and then
seeking a leader to deliver you back into slavery? As
ridiculous as this may sound, this is what happens when
the Lord delivers you, and then you go back into the
world seeking old acquaintances to usher you back into
your old way of life. When you long for the trashy
traditions of old, you curse yourself and hinder the blessings of God.

For years the children of Israel had prayed for God to
send them a deliverer to take them to their land of
promise. Finally, Moses—the deliverer—arrived, and the
journey began. God allowed them to get a good look at
the land where He had led them. But because giants
inhabited their promise, the children of Israel defiled
the blessing of God with murmuring and complaining.

Remember that no great blessing will come without a
fight. If you're not ready to do warfare for some of the
things for which you are seeking God, then you have
already relinquished your rights to freedom and have
chosen to remain a slave to your Egyptian experience. If
the Lord has given you a glimpse of your destiny, never
allow yourself to curse the blessing by murmuring and
complaining. As you will learn in the upcoming chapter,
words have as much power as your actions. So speak
and act only according to the Word of God.

For by your words you will be justified, and by your words you will be condemned.

—Matthew 12:37

Three

Creepy Curses

M any phrases we use have become such an integral part of our daily vocabulary that we are often left dumbfounded concerning some of the things that tend to befall us. Here are some of the phrases we use:

- "If it wasn't for bad luck, I'd have no luck at all."
- "If it isn't one thing, it's another."
- "I'm broke."
- "I can't."

... and the list goes on and on.

We try to justify our use of these words by making excuses: "It's just a figure of speech." Well, it is our "speech" upon which Jesus focuses continually throughout the Bible. Words are powerful. Proverbs tells us, "A man's stomach shall be satisfied from the fruit of his mouth; from the produce of his lips he shall be filled. Death and life are in the power of the tongue, and those who love it will eat its fruit" (Prov. 18:20–21).

With your words, you control the feast that is spread before you. If what you have been digesting lately leaves you with indigestion, simply check out the ingredients that have been coming out of your mouth.

THINK BEFORE YOU SPEAK

> Even so the tongue is a little member and boasts great things. See how great a forest a little fire kindles!
>
> —JAMES 3:5

When the pressures of life add fuel to your emotional furnace, always resist the temptation of spewing out self-inflicting curses that will linger long after the trial has been extinguished. Job experienced this test. After he had lost everything—and he still remained in the midst of a trial that seemed unwilling to throw in the towel—Job *cursed his day:* "So they [his three "friends"] sat down with him on the ground seven days and seven nights, and no one spoke a word to him, for they saw that his grief was very great. After this opened Job his mouth, and *cursed the day of his birth*" (Job 2:13–3:1, emphasis added).

All of us are vulnerable to the trap of self-inflicted curses. Job was a man "blameless and upright, and one who feared God and shunned evil" (Job 1:1). Yet, when he found himself stuck in a seemingly unbearable time, he cursed the day he was born.

And Job spoke, and said:

"May the day perish on which I was born,
And the night in which it was said,
'A male child is conceived.'
May that day be darkness;
May God above not seek it,
Nor the light shine upon it.
May darkness and the shadow of death claim it;
May a cloud settle on it;
May the blackness of the day terrify it.
As for that night, may darkness seize it;
May it not rejoice among the days of the year,
May it not come into the number of the months.
Oh, may that night be barren!
May no joyful shout come into it!
May those curse it who curse the day,
Those who are ready to arouse Leviathan.
May the stars of its morning be dark;
May it look for light, but have none,
And not see the dawning of the day."

—Job 3:2–9

Because our flesh is weak, it surrenders under the burdensome pressures that often befall it. In times of crisis it becomes easier to speak a curse—what we are thinking—rather than to invoke the blessing of the Lord over the situation by applying the Word of God and casting down every stronghold.

Just because the enemy shows you your demise does not mean that you have to believe him, nor do you have to receive his lie as truth. Matthew 11:12 admonishes, "The kingdom of heaven suffers violence, and the violent take it by force." When the devil sees something that he wants, he doesn't ask your permission for it—he simply goes after it. Unless you put up some resistance, he simply snatches it away from you.

BLESSINGS OR CURSES?

Blessed be the God and Father of our Lord Jesus Christ, who has blessed us with every spiritual blessing in the heavenly places in Christ.
—EPHESIANS 1:3

Before the foundation of the world, we inherited the blessings of God. The enemy, however, comes to revoke those blessings and to replace them with curses. We see an interesting illustration of the importance of blessings—and of curses—in the family of Isaac.

Just because the enemy shows you your demise does not mean that you have to believe him, nor do you have to receive his lie as truth.

When Isaac reached old age and knew that he was nearing death, he decided to bless his eldest son, Esau. This blessing was an oral transfer of property and authority to his eldest child and carried legal authority. Calling Esau to his side, he said, "Make me savory food, such as I love, and bring it to me that I may eat, that my soul may bless you before I die" (Gen. 27:4). Rebekah, Jacob and Esau's mother, heard the conversation between Esau and his father and decided to take advantage of this situation by revoking the eldest-child blessings from Esau and placing them instead upon her younger son Jacob, whom she favored. By taking the time to create such an elaborate scheme of manipulation, Rebekah had to have known the tremendous power of blessings and curses. She knew also of the spiritual power that Isaac possessed, enabling him to invoke such blessings.

Today, many of us daily miss out on our blessings because we fail to realize the power of a spoken word. Church has become so ritualistic that the words "God bless you" are nothing more than a cliché that no one really takes seriously. For many Christians, it simply means "hello" and "good-bye."

However, Isaac's family understood the power of blessings to change lives. Jacob took the power of blessings and curses so seriously that he was afraid to deceive his father for fear he would subject himself to a curse. "Look, Esau my brother is a hairy man, and I am a smooth-skinned man. Perhaps my father will feel me, and I shall seem to be a deceiver to him; and I shall bring a curse on myself and not a blessing" (vv. 11–12).

Rebekah consoled Jacob by initiating a self-inflicted curse: "But his mother said to him, 'Let your curse be on me, my son; only obey my voice, and go, get them [two goats] for me'" (v. 13). Later, when it became necessary for Jacob to flee to Haran because of Esau's hatred for him, Scripture indicates that Rebekah had little regard for her own life, perhaps the result of her self-inflicted curse. "And Rebekah said to Isaac, 'I am weary of my life because of the daughters of Heth; if Jacob takes a wife of the daughters of Heth, like these who are the daughters of the land, what good will my life be to me?'" (v. 46).

As the story of Jacob's deception reveals, Isaac had grown old and could no longer rely on his sight, so he depended solely on his senses of touch, smell and hearing. Any time the devil seeks to invoke a curse, he first blinds your spiritual vision, forcing you to rely solely on your natural senses and inclinations. It is crucial, especially during the most critical times in your life, that you do not depend on your natural senses, but rather use the eyes of God.

When Jacob came claiming to be Esau, Isaac responded, "The voice is Jacob's voice, but the hands are the hands of Esau" (v. 22). Rebekah had cunningly placed the skin of goats upon the hands of Jacob and instructed him to wear Esau's clothing so that Isaac would mistake Jacob for Esau.

In the next few passages, we read the execution of Rebekah and Jacob's deceptive plan:

> And he did not recognize him, because his hands were hairy like his brother Esau's hands; so he blessed him. Then he said, "Are you really my son Esau?"
>
> He said, "I am."
>
> He said, "Bring it near to me, and I will eat of my son's game, so that my soul may bless you." So he brought it near to him, and he ate; and he brought him wine, and he drank. Then his father Isaac said to him, "Come near now and kiss me, my son." And he came near and kissed him; and he smelled the smell of his clothing, and blessed him and said:
>
> "Surely, the smell of my son

Is like the smell of a field
Which the LORD has blessed."

—GENESIS 27:23–27

How different the outcome of the story might have been if Isaac, instead of asking Jacob, "Are you really my son Esau?", would have asked that question of God. However, finally convinced by Jacob, Isaac gave in and blessed Jacob:

Therefore may God give you
Of the dew of heaven,
Of the fatness of the earth,
And plenty of grain and wine.
Let peoples serve you,
And nations bow down to you.
Be master over your brethren,
And let your mother's sons bow down to you.
Cursed be everyone who curses you,
And blessed be those who bless you!

—GENESIS 27:28–29

Jacob had just left his father's presence, taking the blessing with him, when Esau entered his father's tent with the savory food Isaac had asked him to make for him. Immediately Isaac realized his mistake. A powerful truth behind the blessing is revealed in the following passage of Scripture:

And his father Isaac said to him, "Who are you?"

So he said, "I am your son, your firstborn, Esau."

Then Isaac trembled exceedingly, and said, "Who? Where is the one who hunted game and

47

brought it to me? I ate all of it before you came, and
I have blessed him—*and indeed he shall be blessed.*"
—GENESIS 27:32–33, EMPHASIS ADDED

Although the wrong person was blessed, *the blessing
could not be revoked.* When a blessing is pronounced
upon an individual by someone who is being used as the
voice of God, the blessing is irrevocable. (See Romans
11:29.) So not only had Jacob succeeded in tricking
Esau out of his birthright, but also he had now deceived
him out of his blessing.

Esau pleaded with his father somehow to find a
blessing for him. Isaac replied with four blessings over
Esau that would affect the course of history:

> And Esau said to his father, "Have you only one
> blessing, my father? Bless me—me also, O my
> father!" And Esau lifted up his voice and wept.
>
> Then Isaac his father answered and said to him:
>
> "Behold, your dwelling shall be of the fatness of
> the earth,
> And of the dew of heaven from above.
> By your sword you shall live,
> And you shall serve your brother;
> And it shall come to pass, when you become rest-
> less,
> That you shall break his yoke from your neck."
> —GENESIS 27:38–40

Throughout history, many reports have been done
regarding inexplicable curses upon individuals, families
and nations. Even in our present day, many people still
allude to family curses, as in the oft-heard references to

"the Kennedy curse" or to curses upon nations, such as we hear said about some of the desperately needy African nations.

POLAR OPPOSITES

> Like a flitting sparrow, like a flying swallow, so a curse without cause shall not alight.
>
> —PROVERBS 26:2

Although both Jacob and Esau were blessed, the deception used to invoke the blessing also invoked somewhat of a curse. Much of the disunity and wars going on in the world today can be traced back in history to this conflict between the two sons of Isaac.

It is important to recognize that a curse carries the same power as a blessing. In Genesis 27:29 we read that when Isaac blessed Jacob, he also incorporated a curse within the blessing: "Cursed be everyone who curses you, and blessed be those who bless you!"

The first step to destroying a curse is to identify its cause. Can you imagine the countless generations that have been cursed simply because someone tried to curse the lineage of Jacob? The power behind both blessings and curses is authority. God has given mankind the power and the authority to invoke a blessing or a curse. But He has also given man the right to choose which will operate in his own life.

> I call heaven and earth as witnesses today against you, that I have set before you life and death, blessing and cursing; therefore choose life, that both you and your descendants may live.
>
> —DEUTERONOMY 30:19

49

The decisions that you make in life affect not only you as an individual—they affect your seed as well. It is for that reason that God admonishes us to "choose life" (blessing), so that both you and your seed will be able to live.

A curse carries the same power as a blessing.

Believe it or not, the Bible does record God-appointed curses. The origin of many of our present-day curses is derived from the Book of Genesis, which means "generation" or "creation"—the origin of all things.

In Genesis 3, curses were pronounced over the serpent for deceiving Adam and Eve:

> So the LORD God said to the serpent:

> "Because you have done this,
> You are cursed more than all cattle,
> And more than every beast of the field;
> On your belly you shall go,
> And you shall eat dust
> All the days of your life.
> And I will put enmity
> Between you and the woman,
> And between your seed and her Seed;
> He shall bruise your head,
> And you shall bruise His heel."
> —GENESIS 3:14–15

God also pronounced a curse over Adam and Eve because of their disobedience:

To the woman He said:

"I will greatly multiply your sorrow and your con-
    ception;
In pain you shall bring forth children;
Your desire shall be for your husband,
And he shall rule over you."

Then to Adam He said, "Because you have heeded
the voice of your wife, and have eaten from the tree
of which I commanded you, saying, 'You shall not
eat of it':

"Cursed is the ground for your sake;
In toil you shall eat of it
All the days of your life.
Both thorns and thistles it shall bring forth for you,
And you shall eat the herb of the field.
In the sweat of your face you shall eat bread
Till you return to the ground,
For out of it you were taken;
For dust you are,
And to dust you shall return."

—GENESIS 3:16–19

In order to understand the supernatural, you must
first understand that many things in the earth operate as
opposites to something else. The opposite of *skinny* is
fat; the opposite of *hot* is *cold*; the opposite of *in* is *out*;
and the opposite of *blessing* is *curse*.

Satan has always tried to clone God by using counter-
feits. Whatever God has, Satan has a counterfeit
co-conspirator. God is the *Father*; Satan is the *father of
lies*. God has a *Son*; Satan has a *son of perdition*, named

51

the antichrist. God has the *Holy Spirit;* Satan has *the unholy spirit*—demons.

Just so, a *curse* is the opposite of a *blessing.* Satan wants you to believe the opposite of the truth; he wants you to believe his lie. He wants you to believe the lie that a curse, something that is normally spoken against you, is something that you have no choice but to live with—and that is a lie. A curse can be reversed by confessing who God says you are, not who Satan says you are.

However, before you can renounce a curse, you must be able to recognize the evidence of a curse and apply the Word of God in order to be set free. The following chart shows the major evidences that a curse is in operation, as well as a Scripture verse with the opposite biblical principle:

EVIDENCE OF A CURSE

1 Continual thoughts of suicide and depression—"I have come that they may have life, and that they may have it more abundantly" (John 10:10).

2 Inability to pay bills, despite having adequate income—"Give, and it will be given to you: good measure, pressed down, shaken together, and running over will be put into your bosom. For with the same measure that you use, it will be measured back to you" (Luke 6:38).

3 Mental and emotional breakdown—"You will keep him in perfect peace, whose mind is stayed on You, because he trusts in You. Trust in the Lord forever, for in YAH, the LORD, is everlasting strength" (Isa. 26:3–4).

4 Multiple miscarriages—"Then God blessed them, and God said to them, 'Be fruitful and multiply; fill the earth and subdue it'" (Gen. 1:28). "And He will love you and bless you and multiply you; He will also bless the fruit of your womb" (Deut. 7:13).

5 Accident prone—"No evil shall befall you, nor shall any plague come near your dwelling; for He shall give His angels charge over you, to keep you in all your ways. In their hands they shall bear you up, lest you dash your foot against a stone" (Ps. 91:10–12).

What continues to energize most curses is the belief of those who authenticate what was spoken while the curse continues to manifest in the natural. In the United States today, there are a number of curses currently recorded in the media and in printed materials that continue to baffle even the most profound skeptics.

For instance, the White House curse began in 1840 with the death of President William H. Harrison, who died of pneumonia. For more than a century after his death, every president elected to office during a year ending in zero died while in office. Because the deaths occurred every twenty years, it was dubbed the "twenty-year curse." The presidents who died in office include William H. Harrison, elected 1840; Abraham Lincoln, elected 1880; William McKinley, elected 1900; Warren Harding, elected 1920; Franklin D. Roosevelt, elected 1940; and John F. Kennedy, elected 1960. Twenty years later an attempt was made on the life of President Ronald Reagan, elected 1980, who miraculously survived the attack. His survival was said to have broken the curse.

A Family Affair

Another very celebrated curse in American culture is the Kennedy curse. The misfortunes and tragedies that have followed the Kennedy family loom as an inevitable decree over their existence—blessed in a very cursed way. Tragedies, accidental deaths, sicknesses and run-ins with the law seem to gleam above the popularity of their family's success.

Unless we identify the curse, denounce it and abide under the covering of God, the curse continues to linger from generation to generation.

We can all cite weaknesses in our families that seem to follow us throughout our lives. No matter how hard we try to shake it, the possibility of a family curse continues to be the nagging nemesis that controls our movements and defines our limitations. These family curses include drug addiction, lawlessness, recurring tragedies and inherited illnesses. Is it the unfortunate hand of fate, or is it the *acceptable curse* that we've packaged as a decree over our lives?

Proverbs 26:2 says, "Like a flitting sparrow, like a flying swallow, so a curse without cause shall not alight." Whether it's the door we have cracked open to create it or our belief in the curse that causes it to linger, curses are very real. But they are also very preventable. Many family curses exist, not because of something that we have done, but because of something *we haven't done.* They may, in some instances, be due to the sins of our forefathers. Unless we identify the curse, renounce it and abide under the covering of God, the curse continues to linger from generation to generation. It becomes the unwelcome yet unchallenged opponent that hinders our growth and potential, the glass ceiling that dictates our boundaries and points out our limitations.

For years I resided under my own family curse of drug addiction, lawlessness, poverty and abuse. I came from a family reared in the hard-core streets known as the Red Hook Projects in Brooklyn, New York. In that environment, taking what you needed was the order of the day—a survival of the fittest. My constant run-ins with the law caught up with me, landing me in the notorious Rikers Island Prison, where God would finally get His *yes* out of me.

Prison became my processing chamber and place of brokenness. There was no one left to lean on except the arms of God, which is right where He wanted me to be. Although the full manifestation of the miracle would not take place until years later, this place of bondage—a prison cell—was the place God used to set me free and propel me into future success. Without a doubt, the curse has now been broken over my family. The blessings of God are now able to reign over my children and my children's children for generations to come.

Regardless of your family's history, you control the acceptable or unacceptable decree that has been pronounced over your future. If inexplicable, recurring experiences continue to hover over your family's existence, release the power through prayer to set your family free. No matter how creepy the curse may seem, you possess the power in your mouth through prayer to destroy every curse in the name of Jesus!

For I am persuaded that neither death nor life, nor
angels nor principalities nor powers, nor things present
nor things to come, nor height nor depth, nor any
other created thing, shall be able to separate us from
the love of God which is in Christ Jesus our Lord.

———————

—ROMANS 8:38–39

Four

Breaking the Curse

One night years ago, while writing my book *Witchcraft in the Pews,* I came to understand the true meaning of deliverance and the power of God to do what He wanted to do when and where He wants to do it. In the previous chapters we learned that the curse of ungodly tradition can build a great wall separating bondage and deliverance. I had demolished that wall years earlier, but I was about to receive another level of deliverance in an area where I didn't even realize I was hindered by a bondage.

As I prepared to work on my book, because I had already preached a message titled "Witchcraft in the Pews," I figured the best way to write the book was to listen to the message again. However, I noticed that every time I listened to one particular part of the tape that dealt with generational curses, I became extremely ill. I would become nauseous and have to rush to the restroom time and time again. I would sit on the bathroom floor for a moment, go back to listen to the tape, and again I would become ill.

Then it hit me. This was more than a coincidence. I was about to be delivered by the same message that God had used to deliver others. As the Lord began to speak to me, I immediately began to pray. As the presence of the Lord filled the room, I was delivered and set free by the power of God. Without the touch of man, without any fanfare or emotionalism, I was taken to another level of understanding and intimacy with the Lord. Eventually, I completed the book, and it became a national bestseller.

You must understand that abstinence is not deliverance.

The spirit realm consists of both blessings and curses. Blessings produce positive results, and curses produce negative results. Both blessings and curses extend not only to a single individual, but also throughout generations and nations.

Perhaps you have been shocked to find something that you thought you were delivered from reappear in your life at the most inopportune time. It rests as a thorn in your flesh to remind you of your weaknesses and proclivities. You must understand that *abstinence* is not *deliverance*. Many people mistakenly believe that just because they go a length of time without indulging in forbidden sins or acquiescing to the temptation that once called their name, they are delivered. Often the weaknesses simply stop calling for a season, but what happens when they begin to ring your line again? Will you answer? Will you pretend not to hear the call? Or will you confront the nagging temptation to disconnect the line permanently?

Many of us make a mistake by pretending not to hear the call. We suppress the obvious problem, put our hands over our eyes and flee to a corner until we can't take it anymore. It is at that moment that either we give in to the recurring curse or we call out to God for help.

More often than not, suppression will cause you to answer the call rather than to disconnect the line and walk in the liberty of peace you are entitled to enjoy.

> Submit to God. Resist the devil and he will flee from you.
>
> —JAMES 4:7

We often quote the latter part of this scripture—"Resist the devil *and he will flee*"—while leaving out the former part, which says, "Submit to God." This is a two-part command. It becomes very difficult to resist the devil without first submitting to God, especially when the enemy has all of the information he needs concerning the curse that continues to haunt you and the weaknesses from which you find it impossible to flee.

Regardless of how intricate and unyielding a curse may seem, know that Jesus bore the curse so that you could receive the blessing.

> For He made Him who knew no sin to be sin for us, that we might become the righteousness of God in Him.
>
> —2 CORINTHIANS 5:21

Jesus became sin so that you could be set free and become "the righteousness of God." Even in the case of an unknown curse that is lingering in your life, the Holy Spirit will lead you and guide you, revealing the hidden hindrances in your life that prevent the full manifestation of victory in your life.

GETTING RID OF THE CURSE

If while reading this book you discover that you have been living below your spiritual blessing because of a hidden curse, do something about it—submit it to God. Then you will be able to experience a life of victory as a believer.

Consider these three important principles as you begin to submit fully to God:

1. The power of confession

> That if you confess with your mouth the Lord Jesus and believe in your heart that God has raised Him from the dead, you will be saved.
> —ROMANS 10:9

The power of confession does not apply only to salvation. It is just as powerful when petitioning God for deliverance from cultural curses and unconfessed sins.

If you have been battling recurring habits, pray the following prayer, inserting whatever applies to your particular experience within the blanks:

> *Dear Father, I confess You as Lord in my life and over my life. I believe that You died on the cross and became sin so that I may be set free. Now Lord, I ask You to deliver me*

*from this recurring weakness and sin of
_____. I renounce this
curse of _____ in my life.
I submit myself to You so that Your will may
be done in my life, here on earth as it is
already done in heaven. I thank You and
give You praise for my deliverance, right
now, in the name of Jesus! Amen.*

2. Close the door to curse in your life

Like a flitting sparrow, like a flying swallow, so a
curse without cause shall not alight.

—PROVERBS 26:2

Whether you are aware of it or not, there is no curse
present in your life without a cause. Repent of all open
doors to the demonic—harboring unforgiveness, dabbling in the occult, rebellion, disobedience, hatred,
bitterness and so on.

3. Exercise faith

Therefore I say to you, whatever things you ask
when you pray, believe that you receive them, and
you will have them.

—MARK 11:24

Jesus has issued to each of us a measure of faith to
receive deliverance, walk out of bondage and enjoy the
fruits of being set free. "Therefore if the Son makes you
free, you shall be free indeed" (John 8:36). Exercise
your faith, believe that you have received from Him the
gift of life and freedom from curses, and be set free
indeed!

With deliverance comes a change in lifestyle. During the rehabilitation process, a recovering addict is taught the importance of finding new friends and, when necessary, the necessity of changing his or her environment in order to stay clean. As it is in the natural, so goes it in the spiritual. You alone will know what changes you need to make in your life in order to "stay clean" and to maintain your deliverance.

> You will keep him in perfect peace,
> Whose mind is stayed on You,
> Because he trusts in You.
> Trust in the LORD forever,
> For in YAH, the LORD, is everlasting strength.
> —ISAIAH 26:3–4

Keep your mind on Christ, and allow Him to be the source of your strength. When you realize the significance of deliverance as opposed to abstinence, you release the blessings of God in your life and destroy the curse.

THE POSITIVE EFFECT OF A BLESSING

It is often considered taboo to discuss the subject of curses in great detail, but it is a matter that affects entire families and even generations, and it must be addressed. Though we don't often hear about curses, the nature of curses or their causes, the Bible has much to say about them.

Although we may not understand completely what curses are about, we should not lack the desire to learn more about such great hindrances so that we can identify them, destroy them over our lives and walk in freedom and victory. We must come to the realization that it is often the curse that limits or hinders the blessings of God over our lives.

With deliverance comes a change in lifestyle.

Both blessings and curses are words that are spoken with authority over an individual's life, causing either a negative or positive effect. As I said earlier, the opposite of a blessing is a curse. They're both similar, in that both can last for generations.

As we journey in time, you will notice that much of today's focus is going back to its origin, the Middle East. Ultimately the focus will come full circle to its completion through the Book of Revelation. As we have already stated, the cycle begins in the Book of Genesis:

Now the LORD had said unto Abram:

"Get out of your country,
From your family
And from your father's house,
To a land that I will show you.
I will make you a great nation;
I will bless you
And make your name great;
And you shall be a blessing.
I will bless those who bless you,
And I will curse him who curses you;
And in you all the families of the earth shall be
   blessed."

—GENESIS 12:1–3

These verses are God's promise to Abraham—a sevenfold promise. There are seven specific blessings spoken over the life of Abraham in these three verses. If Abraham will obey the voice of God by getting out of the country and away from his kindred, these blessings will be his.

Be aware that some curses will never be broken in your life until you first distance yourself from those who are comfortable with your bondage. Let's look at this sevenfold blessing to Abraham:

THE SEVENFOLD BLESSING

1 God will make Abraham a great nation—
"I will make you a great nation."

2 He will bless Abraham—
"I will bless you."

3 He will make Abraham's name great—
"…and make your name great."

4 Abraham will be a blessing—
"And you shall be a blessing."

5 God promises to bless those who bless Abraham—"I will bless those who bless you."

6 He promises to curse those who curse Abraham—"And I will curse him who curses you." (This is a blessing to Abraham and instant curse to those who curse him.)

7 In Abraham, all the families of the earth will be blessed—"And in you all the families of the earth shall be blessed."

REASONS FOR CURSES

There are several things that can account for a curse. The more you remain oblivious to these things, the wider the door opens, giving you room to walk into it. When we consider the lineage of Abraham, it is amazing to imagine the countless number of individuals who are walking around cursed simply because they cursed Abraham and his descendants. Let's investigate some of the known causes of curses according to Deuteronomy 27:15–26.

Dabbling in the occult

> Cursed is the one who makes a carved or molded image, an abomination to the LORD, the work of the hands of the craftsman, and sets it up in secret.
> —DEUTERONOMY 27:15

Many are cursed for dabbling in the occult or placing other things before the true and living God. Many generations have been cursed because their grandparents practiced witchcraft, ancient healing methods, voodoo and ungodly cultic ceremonies that they dismissed as spiritual and godly worship. The Lord is a jealous God, and He will not share His worship with other gods. This includes secret trinkets that we use as good luck charms for wealth, health and so on. We will look closer at how we open the door to the occult in the next section.

Not honoring father and mother

> Cursed is the one who treats his father or his mother with contempt.
>
> —DEUTERONOMY 27:16

Exodus 20:12 warns us, "Honor your father and your mother, that your days may be long upon the land which the LORD your God is giving you." Regardless of what the case may be, we are to respect our parents to avoid being cursed. I often tell a single mother to teach her sons and daughters to respect their father, whether he is a vital part of their lives or not. Likewise, I encourage fathers to teach their children to address their mother properly and to maintain respect for her.

In today's society of absentee and drug-addicted parents, the last recommendation many children want to hear is to "respect." Although you may have a very "valid" reason for lacking respect, the rule remains, and there are no exceptions. If you want the blessings of the Lord to reign in your life, regardless of how old you are, respect your parents and enjoy the benefits of a lengthened life.

Mistreatment of a neighbor

> Cursed is the one who moves his neighbor's land-
> mark.
>
> —DEUTERONOMY 27:17

We are commanded in Luke 10:27 to "love the Lord your God with all your heart, with all your soul, with all your strength, and with all your mind, *and your neighbor as yourself*" (emphasis added). How many of us are cursed for the malicious behavior we inflict upon each other on a daily basis?

Taking advantage of another

> Cursed is the one who makes the blind to wander
> off the road.
>
> —DEUTERONOMY 27:18

This refers to taking advantage of the vulnerability of another individual. There are millions of people walking around who think that they have gotten away with culpable acts against those whom they have misled. This scripture, however, warns us of the curse to follow. Proverbs 17:13 also sends a very sobering warning: "Whoever rewards evil for good, evil will not depart from his house." How many individuals have cursed their own homes by repaying the good of others with evil?

Misleading others

> Cursed is the one who perverts the justice due the
> stranger, the fatherless, and widow.
>
> —DEUTERONOMY 27:19

This again refers to misleading others purposely. Whether you know the individual or not, to intentionally deceive another individual makes you vulnerable to a curse.

Incest

> Cursed is the one who lies with his father's wife, because he has uncovered his father's bed.
> —DEUTERONOMY 27:20

I often pray for individuals at the altar who have been the victims of incest. Not only does a curse come upon the perpetrator of the incest, but unfortunately, through no fault of his or her own, the victim is often cursed as well. Victims of incest might go for years without understanding why they struggle with certain bondages such as promiscuity, rage or sexual immorality—all residual effects of lost innocence because of a spirit of transfer through sexual contact with a perverse individual.

> Cursed is the one who lies with his sister, the daughter of his father or the daughter of his mother...Cursed is the one who lies with his mother-in-law.
> —DEUTERONOMY 27:22–23

Again, Scripture warns against incest—mothers-in-law included.

Bestiality

> Cursed is the one who lies with any kind of animal.
> —DEUTERONOMY 27:21

70

Amazingly enough, bestiality is very common today, especially with those involved in the occult. Its origin, however, dates back throughout the centuries, and it has always invoked a curse.

Violence and murder

> Cursed is the one who attacks his neighbor secretly...Cursed is the one who takes a bribe to slay an innocent person.
>
> —DEUTERONOMY 27:24–25

Believe it or not, the Bible not only unveils the curse for murderers, but for those who murder for cash as well—modern-day hit men.

Lawbreakers

> Cursed is the one who does not confirm all the words of this law by observing them.
>
> —DEUTERONOMY 27:26

IGNORANCE IS NO EXCUSE

You may be ignorant of the law, or you may disagree with the law, *but no one is exempt from the law.* For that reason it is important for you to examine your own attitudes and behaviors. You may discover the nature of the curse that has been your nagging nemesis. You may also be wondering, "In what other areas can a Christian unknowingly live a defeated life?" Because my ministry is one of deliverance, there are often demonic manifestations that occur during the services in which I minister throughout the country. People are often baffled as to why and how a Christian can be bound. There are several reasons that could account for why an individual who professes salvation is under demonic or ungodly influences. These reasons include the following three things:

1. Ignorance

As previously stated, ignorance of the law is no excuse. Many Christians are unaware of the many curses that they invoke upon themselves due to their behavior, moral turpitude and ignorance.

2. Opening the door to the occult

Whether you have been involved in seances or other ungodly rituals, dabbling with the occult is as dangerous as being fully immersed in the occult. There are many ways to open the door to the occult, including tattooing the body, body piercings, wearing satanic jewelry and participating in satanic games such as the Ouija board, Dungeons and Dragons and other ungodly games.

You may be ignorant of the law,
or you may disagree with the law,
but no one is exempt from the law.

But this does not mean you are doomed or condemned if you have permanently tattooed your body or done other things to it. John 3:17 reminds us, "For God did not send His Son into the world to condemn the world, but that the world through Him might be saved." Especially in today's generation of cyberspace and the imaginary world of Game Boys, Nintendos and PlayStations, which have become the babysitters of the twenty-first century, parents must use careful wisdom when choosing the games their children are allowed to play. Parents must be aware of how their children's actions today will affect their actions tomorrow.

3. Breaking vows and/or withholding from God that which is His

> Will a man rob God?
> Yet you have robbed Me!
> But you say,
> "In what way have we robbed you?"
> In tithes and offerings.
> You are cursed with a curse,
> For you have robbed Me,
> Even this whole nation.
>
> —MALACHI 3:9

There are certain vows that we make that, when broken, will cause self-inflicted curses. "When you make a vow to the LORD your God, you shall not delay to pay it; for the LORD your God will surely require it of you, and it would be sin to you" (Deut. 23:21).

Some curses are spoken with such authority that they will most certainly come to pass. In 2 Samuel 3, David spoke a curse over his cousin Joab for murdering Abner. Abner was Saul's commander in chief and the one who brought David before Saul after David had slain the giant Goliath. David mourned the death of Abner. Realizing the greatness of Abner, David immediately renounced the curse of Abner's death from his own life and instead pronounced it upon Abner's murderer, Joab. Understanding the nature of curses and the effect they have over entire households, David not only renounced the curse over himself, but also over his entire kingdom. He transferred the curse to Joab and "all his father's house."

> Afterward, when David heard it, he said, "My kingdom and I are guiltless before the LORD forever of the blood of Abner the son of Ner. Let it rest on the head of Joab and on all his father's house; and let there never fail to be in the house of Joab one who has a discharge or is a leper, who leans on a staff or falls by the sword, or who lacks bread."
>
> —2 SAMUEL 3:28–29

In 1 Kings 2:27–31, we read that years later this curse befell Joab. By the order of David's son King Solomon, Joab is slain at the altar of the tabernacle by Solomon's commander in chief, Benaiah. David had immediate foreknowledge of the curse, but he was wise enough to divert it from himself and his kingdom. Joab had the opportunity to fulfill the means to a great future and to have generations of his lineage blessed, but because of the evil that he committed he was cursed. Much like the fig tree in Mark 11, Joab showed potential. But when the time came to deliver, he was unable to produce the fruit.

CURSE OF THE FIG TREE

Showing great potential is not a guarantee of future success. Making the wrong decisions will cause you to curse the seed that has been planted inside of you and to abort your own destiny.

In Mark 11, Jesus saw a fig tree afar off. He was hungry, so He approached the fig tree, but He noticed that the tree had only leaves, "for it was not the season for figs" (v. 13). In response, Jesus cursed the fig tree.

The tree appeared to produce, but upon further investigation it was found lacking fruit. Let's liken this story to going to the grocery store. You pull into the parking lot where you see posters decorating the store windows to advertise all of the current sales. The lights are on, the "Open" sign flashes in the window, and the word "Welcome" meets you at the doors as they slide open to allow your entry. However, when you get inside, the shelves are bare; there's no food in the store at all.

The store gave the appearance of being able to meet your need, but it left you hungering for what it could not produce. How many times have you hungered for the Word of God, yet continued to starve to death because the leader you trusted to give you direction and clarity appeared to be productive but lacked the fruit necessary to satisfy your spiritual appetite? Or how many times have you remained hungry because you could not prioritize your life to the place where you had a consistent time to spend reading the Word of God and allowing God to give you revelation from His Word?

In our story about the fig tree, the day after Jesus had cursed the tree, as He and His disciples passed the tree, they noticed that it had "dried up from the roots" (v. 20). Peter responded, "Rabbi, look! The fig tree which You cursed has withered away" (v. 21).

"Well, of course it has," Jesus responded. Then He instructed them:

Have faith in God. For assuredly, I say to you, whoever says to this mountain, "Be removed and be cast into the sea," and does not doubt in his heart, but believes that those things he says will be done, he will have whatever he says.

—MARK 11:22–23

Once again, this affirms the power of the spoken word of faith.

SATANIC CURSES

Satan heavily influences many curses. On a daily basis, witches, warlocks and everyday folks speak curses against each other, which, if not renounced, affect entire families. Notice that cussing at an individual is simply using foul language and derogatory words, but cursing a person leaves mental and emotional scarring that can take years to overcome.

As children we used to quote, "Stick and stones may break my bones, but words will never hurt me." Well, that statement could not be further from the truth. Actually, words, when spoken with authority, can have debilitating effects on an individual's life. However, just because a person speaks a curse over your life does not mean that you have to accept it. Renounce the curse, and do as the Bible instructs: "Bless those who curse you, and pray for those who spitefully use you" (Luke 6:28).

Blessing those who curse us can be a real chore. But the Bible doesn't instruct us, "Curse those who curse us." Nor does it say, "Retaliate against those who render evil for our good." Rather, the Word of God is very clear in its instruction to us. In Romans 12:19–21,

Paul tells us how to behave when we are faced with people who curse us with their words or behavior:

> Beloved, do not avenge yourselves, but rather give place to wrath; for it is written, "Vengeance is Mine, I will repay," says the Lord. Therefore "if your enemy is hungry, feed him; if he is thirsty, give him a drink; for in so doing you will heap coals of fire on his head." Do not be overcome by evil, but overcome evil with good.

The enemy has successfully convinced some people that his power is stronger than the power of God. The Lord and those who serve Him wholeheartedly, however, know better. The Word of God teaches us that "the weapons of our warfare are not carnal..." (2 Cor. 10:4). Why, then, would we attempt to defeat the satanic influences of Satan by carnal means? It is not by our own power that we win the war, but it is the power of God that smites the forces of evil and causes those who obey the voice of the Lord to rejoice in victory.

God knows that our natural inclination as human vessels is to strike back. He therefore leaves us several instructions:

> Bless them who persecute you; bless and do not curse.
>
> —ROMANS 12:14

> ...not returning evil for evil or reviling for reviling, but on the contrary blessing, knowing that you were called to this, that you may inherit a blessing.
>
> —1 PETER 3:9

Finally, my brethren, be strong in the Lord and in
the power of His might. Put on the whole armor of
God, that you may be able to stand against the wiles
of the devil. For we do not wrestle against flesh and
blood, but against principalities, against powers,
against the rulers of the darkness of this age, against
spiritual hosts of wickedness in the heavenly places.
—Ephesians 6:10–12

Don't expect that by obeying these commands you
will always change the heart of the person who's cursing
you, but it does place you under the divine covering of
God, which is where you should desire to remain
despite your circumstances.

Words, when spoken with authority, can have debilitating effects on an individual's life.

Curses can come from witches, warlocks, psychics
and other mediums. Believe it or not, they visit our
churches and sit among us—blending in, rejoicing as
we rejoice, while simultaneously cursing the cause of
Christ. Today, the United States is filled with modern-
day witches and warlocks that even Christians have
been known to visit for advice. Visiting psychics and
other satanic mediums invokes self-inflicted curses.

No one can serve two masters; for either he will
hate the one and love the other, or else he will be
loyal to the one and despise the other. You
cannot serve God and mammon.
—Matthew 6:24

Practitioners of the occult are persons who purposely choose to serve Satan. Why, then, would a person who professes the name of Christ seek advice from someone who opposes Him? Countless numbers of people are reeled in on a daily basis because, in seeking direction from these ungodly mediums, they are told exactly what they think they *need* to hear.

You must understand that Satan can and *does* do things for people and foretell things that will come to pass in the person's life. It's the bait he uses to pull individuals further into his trap. His comfort, however, is always short-lived. In order to keep a person in his clutches, he continually uses ungodly sources to steer the individual further and further away from God and into his demonic and manipulative web of darkness and deceit.

> Take heed to yourselves, lest your heart be deceived, and you turn aside and serve other gods and worship them, lest the LORD's anger be aroused against you.
> —DEUTERONOMY 11:16–17

Enemies will always attempt to curse what God has blessed. But it is impossible for the enemy to curse God's blessings in the lives of those who hearken to the voice of God. Our enemies will soon tire and go on their way, seeking a more vulnerable and gullible victim. "Submit to God. Resist the devil and he will flee from you" (James 4:7).

There is an interesting account of a curse that simply would not work in Numbers 23–24. The children of Israel had come to the plains of Moab. Realizing the destruction that the Israelites had brought upon the Amorites, Balak, the king of Moab, was terrified and sent for Balaam, asking that he curse the children of Israel.

Balak was fully aware of the authority of Balaam's blessings and curses. He told Balaam:

> Therefore please come at once, curse this people for me, for they are too mighty for me. Perhaps I shall be able to defeat them and drive them out of the land, for I know that he whom you bless is blessed, and he whom you curse is cursed.
>
> —Numbers 22:6

At Balak's request, three times Balaam tried to curse the children of Israel, with no success. As forewarned by the Lord, Balaam could only speak what God allowed him to speak. Each time he opened his mouth, a blessing came out—not the curse that Balak so desperately desired.

It is impossible for the enemy to curse God's blessings in the lives of those who hearken to the voice of God.

In Numbers 23, Balaam tried to explain to Balak that he was operating under the authority and will of God. No iniquity or perverseness had been found in Jacob and the children of Israel; hence, the blessing of the Lord reigned over them.

> God is not a man, that He should lie, nor a son of
> man, that He should repent. Has He said, and
> will He not do? Or has He spoken, and will He
> not make it good? Behold, I have received a com-
> mand to bless; He has blessed, and I cannot
> reverse it.
>
> —NUMBERS 23:19–20

What a powerful concept! It further proves that what
God has blessed cannot be reversed by mere evildoers
who desire to curse what God desires to be blessed.
God is not like mankind who blesses and curses based
on the emotional state of mind. If God says it, He will
do it. If He speaks it, it will come to pass. The children
of Israel were blessed, and there was nothing that
Balak, king of Moab, or Balaam could do to transform
that blessing into a curse.

There is nothing mysterious about blessings or
curses. The Word of God makes it very plain:

> I have set before you life and death, blessing and
> cursing; therefore choose life, that both you and
> your descendants may live.
>
> —DEUTERONOMY 30:19

Blessings follow in hearkening to the voice of the
Lord. Even in the midst of adversity, the blessings of the
Lord will overtake you. God wants to overwhelm you
with His blessings. He states just a few of those blessings
in the following verses:

DEUTERONOMY 28:3–8

1 "Blessed shall you be in the city, and blessed shall you be in the country" (v. 3).

2 "Blessed shall be the fruit of your body, the produce of your ground and the increase of your herds, the increase of your cattle and the offspring of your flocks" (v. 4).

3 "Blessed shall be your basket and your kneading bowl" (v. 5).

4 "Blessed shall you be when you come in, and blessed shall you be when you go out" (v. 6).

5 "The Lord will cause your enemies who rise against you to be defeated before your face; they shall come out against you one way and flee before you seven ways" (v. 7).

6 "The Lord will command the blessing on you in your storehouses and in all to which you set your hand, and He will bless you in the land which the Lord your God is giving you" (v. 8).

When we don't abide by the stipulations that invoke blessings, the result is a curse.

> But it shall come to pass, if you do not obey the voice of the LORD your God, to observe carefully all His commandments and His statutes which I command you today, *that all these curses will come upon you and overtake you.*
> —DEUTERONOMY 28:15, EMPHASIS ADDED

Identify the curse that has continued to linger, and expunge it from your life once and for all. Hearken to the voice of the Lord, and experience the favor of God upon your life. Remember that we have an adversary who seeks to destroy us through physical and mental suffering. Though there may be a cause for the curse, this doesn't mean that you have to live with the curse. Realizing how blessed you are makes you less vulnerable to a curse. It can be broken simply by speaking the Word of God. Renounce the curse, and confess what God says about you: "You are blessed and not cursed."

Now that you have taken time to identify the demonic influences that have continued to hover over your life, enter into spiritual warfare and reverse the curse, thus invoking the blessings of God:

> *Lord, You have blessed me with all spiritual blessings in heavenly places. Therefore, I declare that I am blessed and not cursed. I renounce the curse(s) of _____ that has (have) lingered over my family and me. I speak forth the blessings of God upon my entire household. I thank You that the*

manifestation of Your blessings shall be a witness to my entire family and to unbelievers alike of Your goodness and Your power. I thank You that even as I pray, not only am I being set free, but also those in my family are being set free by Your power.

Thank You that the favor of God now reigns over my life. I pray that my enlightenment will be increased and my insight sharpened to hear and obey Your voice. No weapon that is formed against me shall prosper. I am blessed and not cursed! In Jesus' name, amen.

But I am afraid, lest as the serpent deceived Eve by his craftiness, your minds should be led astray from the simplicity and purity of devotion to Christ.

—*2 CORINTHIANS 11:3, NAS*

Five

Pentecostal Potholes

I n chapter one we discussed the possibility of suffering in order to reach that place in God where we often long to reside. Paul said it this way:

> And if children, then heirs—heirs of God and joint heirs with Christ, if indeed we suffer with Him, that we may also be glorified together. For I consider that the sufferings of this present time are not worthy to be compared with the glory which shall be revealed in us.
>
> —ROMANS 8:17–18

The problem, however, is that many overzealous warriors in the body of Christ have taken this scripture out of context and used it as a means to exert their authority and control over unsuspecting and vulnerable victims in the body of Christ. When suffering for the

87

sake of Christ, "all things work together for good." But when suffering for man, life becomes a rapid downhill spiral into despair. The best way to ensure your spiritual sanity is to remain in a prayerful mode, judging all things based upon the Word of God, which states, "Men always ought to pray and not lose heart" (Luke 18:1).

If someone is telling you to do something that is causing you to compromise your faith and belief in God, "test the spirits, whether they are of God; because many false prophets have gone out into the world" (1 John 4:1).

> *If we are to avoid the potholes and bottomless pits on the road to victory, we must become wise concerning the devices of Satan.*

Churches today are filled with the horror stories of people who trust a leader to give them direction but who are instead caused to wander in the wilderness and miss out on their promised land. As a youth, I watched a young girl marry the man of her dreams—or so she thought. Early into the marriage the young man became very abusive, often causing her to land in the hospital, incapacitated for days. Because she loved the Lord with all her heart, she dared not make a move without first seeking guidance from her spiritual leader.

The church she attended was very traditional and legalistic. Whenever she sought counsel from her pastor, the advice remained the same: "Submit, and remain with your husband." Because she looked to her pastor as the mouthpiece of God, she did not want to do anything that went against his advice for fear she would risk compromising her relationship with God. Time and time again she returned to an apologetic husband, bearing the brunt of empty promises.

She became his living, breathing punching bag! Still the advice remained the same: "Stay with your husband, pray harder, and have more faith." The last time he beat her, it rendered her unconscious. She did, however, manage to conjure up enough strength to look up from her hospital bed into the eyes of her pastor and speak her dying words: "Pastor, I did what you told me to do."

Throughout my many years of travel, ministers and leaders have often rushed to share with me the latest revelations given to them—they claim—by God. "Listen to this," they explain. "This is something you have never heard before. God gave it to me as a word for the church."

Many times there is no biblical basis to back their newfound revelations. That clues me in immediately to the fact that the "revelations" were not from God. So many zealous warriors in the body of Christ have found themselves in the midst of heated battles because they desired to conquer an unrealistic conquest. They attempted to challenge the enemy's twenty-first-century artillery with puny sticks and spears. If we are to avoid the potholes and bottomless pits on the road to victory, we must become wise concerning the devices of Satan.

THE UNHOLY ANOINTING

In the early days of my church, I began counseling a family regarding problems within their home. One day as I prayed for them in private, I went into a vision that lasted for about twenty to thirty minutes. In my vision I saw something very wrong going on in their home, right under their noses. They were unaware of it at the time.

A woman minister was living in their home. In the vision, I saw that when the family left the house, young women entered the home from the back of the house, coming for private prayer sessions with the woman minister. These prayer sessions included the burning of candles and mystical ceremonial services. She even had the young women strip off all their clothes; then she anointed them with oil from head to toe.

This lady belonged to our church and attended regularly, so one day I decided to confront her regarding her ungodly "services." However, as I was about to approach her about what I had seen, the Holy Spirit stopped me.

One major facet of spiritual warfare is timing. Some people will never experience true intimacy with Christ because they are not able to handle the things that He might show them. Others do not have the ability to wait for His timing before moving forward. So I did as the Holy Spirit had instructed and held my peace, waiting on His timing for confrontation rather than acting out of my own anger.

One of the young ladies who had attended these sessions and been anointed by the woman minister also attended my church, so I decided to share with her what I had seen in the vision. Ironically, before I could even complete my first sentence, she began to shake violently. She broke down in tears as the demonic spirits that had been transferred to her began to manifest.

"Who did this to you?" I asked her, although I already knew the answer. Before she could answer me, I said the name of the woman minister who had been having these private "prayer" sessions. As soon as I said the name, this young woman broke down again and confessed that everything I had said was true.

Finally I received a release from the Lord to confront the woman who was conducting these sessions with what I had seen in my vision. So I did exactly that, telling her everything I had seen in the vision. She admitted that what I had seen was very accurate, but she refused to stop conducting these ungodly sessions. "This is the revelation that the Lord gave me for getting these young women set free," she explained.

Why, then, were they so bound? I knew that there was no biblical basis for what she was doing, and since she would not stop, I advised the family with whom she was living of the dangers of allowing her to remain in their home.

Satan's strategy has always been to complicate the simplicity of the Word of God. He wants the true message of Jesus Christ to be corrupted, hindered and aborted by meaningless verbiage and conjured traditions of men that have no power to effect a change.

While the church remains engaged in heated battles of dos and don'ts, Satan is strategizing to have a field day in the lives of God's people and prevent them from bringing others to Christ. We can become so caught up in debates about divorce, head-coverings, submission, who is and is not filled with the Holy Ghost, who is and isn't saved and so forth that we forget the purpose of the church. Our mandate is this: "Go out into the highways and hedges, and compel them to come in, that my house may be filled" (Luke 14:23).

This mandate says nothing about confusing people with church doctrine first. It simply says, "Tell them to come."

In 2 Corinthians 12:19–20, Paul reminded Christians of the importance of staying focused and of keeping our purpose in perspective:

> Again, do you think that we excuse ourselves to you? We speak before God in Christ. But we do all things, beloved, for your edification. For I fear lest, when I come, I shall not find you such as I wish, and that I shall be found by you such as you do not wish; lest there be contentions, jealousies, outbursts of wrath, selfish ambitions, backbitings, whisperings, conceits, tumults.

Paul reminded the church at Corinth that although everything he did was for their strengthening and edifying, his focus remained on God. He admonished them to remember God in their actions as well. He emphasized their vulnerability and his own potential of being pulled into "contentions, jealousies, outbursts of wrath, selfish ambitions, backbitings, whisperings, conceits, tumults." He warned against these things. Anytime that these types of things are going on in the church, you can rest assured that the people involved in them are not fulfilling God's purpose.

CREATED FOR GOD'S PURPOSE

All things were created by God for His purpose.

> For by Him all things were created that are in heaven and that are on earth, visible and invisible,

> whether thrones or dominions or principalities
> or powers. All things were created through Him
> and for Him.
>
> —COLOSSIANS 1:16

You must understand that you can only produce that which you were created by God to produce, that which is in you. For instance, an iron was created to produce heat to rid clothes of wrinkles; a fan was created to produce cool air to bring comfort and rid us of heat. You wouldn't use an iron to cool off, nor would you use a fan to iron clothes. Both creations were made for a specific purpose.

The electricity that is used to operate both the fan and the iron can be likened to the Holy Spirit. Once the electricity generates through the fan and the iron, they are given the power to perform the task for which they were both created. Likewise, once the electrical current of God's power—the Holy Spirit—hits you, what you were created to perform to His glory will manifest and go forth to accomplish His purpose.

When the anointing of the Lord hits you, you are going to illuminate only the area for which you were created. You can try all day long to operate in an area for which you were not created, but you will only produce self-inflicted frustration. Yet we are often inclined to focus more on *position* than on what we were created to do. There are many people in the body of Christ who push themselves to perform what is not in them to produce. If you were not created by God—anointed by Him—for a certain area of ministry, you will never be able to develop effectively the revelation of that field of ministry. You will never be able to train and excel in that particular level of deliverance because you weren't created for that purpose.

Take the time to understand what you were created to do instead of what you think you should be doing. Be careful to seek the face of the Lord for His instruction and direction concerning spiritual matters. Never cease to seek the Lord concerning His will for your life, even during seasons of stagnation. Be willing to place yourself and your ministry under the authority and spiritual covering of a godly spiritual leader.

> *Never stop doing what you were*
> *called and anointed by God to do.*
> *God cannot bless the life of a slacker.*

Many people are unwilling to place their ministries under authority. Having no one to answer to allows them to do whatever they want to do rather than simply staying focused on what they were created to do. Lacking a covering frees you to set your own standards, mark your own boundaries and, ultimately, *set traps for your own demise.* However, when you place your ministry under sound authority, you will always have a safety net to cushion your fall, giving you the opportunity to recoup, heal the wounded areas and go forth with power. "And let us not grow weary while doing good, for in due season we shall reap if we do not lose heart" (Gal. 6:9).

Regardless of how long it may seem to be before you start to see the fruition of your blessing, never stop doing what you were called and anointed by God to do. God cannot bless the life of a slacker. All too often over the years I have observed lethargic, indecisive people in the body of Christ who profess to have been called to impact nations. This attitude and way of thinking will only prevent the anointing from residing over your ministry and will cause spiritual matters to be concealed from you.

The ways and thoughts of the Lord are much higher than our ways. In order for God to use you, He must have your wholehearted cooperation. You must not develop an opinion about how He should work or in what facet of ministry He should use you.

> "For My thoughts are not your thoughts,
> Nor are your ways My ways," says the LORD.
> "For as the heavens are higher than the earth,
> So are My ways higher than your ways,
> And My thoughts than your thoughts."
> —ISAIAH 55:8–9

Mankind cannot think like God, neither can mankind figure Him out. Once you have developed a permanent opinion about how He operates or have decided that you have Him all figured out, you have set your own limitations. You must remain open to the voice of God at all times without any predetermined ideologies. God demands from you what He created you to produce. Therefore, you must balance your life according to your calling, giving to God unselfishly of yourself and, more importantly, of what lies within you that already belongs to Him.

> Render therefore to Caesar the things that are Caesar's, *and to God the things that are God's.*
> —MATTHEW 22:21, EMPHASIS ADDED

When you are called by God for a specific task, your life cannot be consumed with the things of the world, focusing only on worldly tasks every hour of the day. There must be a commitment on your part to make time for God through study, preparation, listening for His voice and hearkening to His command.

Many times we complain that God is not speaking. In actuality, He has spoken many times, but we were just too busy to pay attention, or we didn't receive the answer from Him that we were expecting. When we're open to the Lord and His voice, we show forth the fruit of His vine rather than the harvest of our own unfruitful plantings.

Remember that every tree bears fruit after its kind. God is the husbandman; we are His fruit, and we are to produce our own fruit. That is why being planted under the proper leadership is very important, especially for those going forth in ministry. If the one leading you does not know how to properly lead you to God or to impart the Word of God within you, then your idea and understanding of true leadership ability will be contorted by fictionalized ideas about how to lead others.

Many conflicts and potholes arise within churches because the pastors and leaders have not spent enough time training the people they have appointed as leaders. They may know each other in the spirit, but it is crucial for those who are serving in a leadership capacity under a church leader to have time to learn that leader's personality, movements, tendencies, attitudes and soft spots. Fellowship affords you the opportunity to see whether or not a person is judgmental, overreactive or suspicious. All of these factors are a part of the revelatory knowledge you need to develop about the person who leads the church in which you serve as a leader.

You need to know if your leader has an ax to grind about a certain issue. You must discern if he or she is heady or high-minded. Does your leader like to boast, or is that person proud, self-righteous or snobbish? Does he exalt himself above others, or has he appointed himself to position?

> *There is no three-step program*
> *to teach spiritual warfare ministry.*
> *The answer is simple: Study the Word*
> *of God, seek His face and remain open*
> *to His voice of authority.*

As a leader equipped with the weapons of warfare, maintain your ability to have a good attitude and self-assurance. Avoid arrogance. Don't entertain a twisted view of others just because you cannot see past their imperfections. Keep in mind that we all have issues with which we must deal continually—including you. It will help to alleviate any temptation to arrogance and self-righteousness. Remember that it is often those who have hidden imperfections who expose and ridicule the imperfections of others.

You may not be experiencing the bondages that you see in the lives of others, but you must be ever mindful of the things from which the Lord has delivered you. He loves those who do not know Him as Lord with the same degree of love by which He loves you.

Let's consider three definitions:

- Attitude—a position assumed for a specific purpose; a mental position with regard to a fact or state; a negative or hostile state of mind; a cocky or arrogant manner

- Self-assurance—being sure of oneself: self-confident

- Confidence—characterized by assurance; self-reliant; trustful, confiding; full of conviction; certain

Good leaders are kind and not overly judgmental. They are not full of vain imaginations. They do not spend the majority of their time watching television or in ungodly fellowship, but they understand that everything must have a balance. Good leaders have great appreciation and concern for themselves and others; they are in touch with their own inner feelings and inner issues. In order to be a good leader with a positive impact on others, you cannot allow "events" or seasons to dictate your happiness. Keeping a well-rounded attitude plays a major part in being able to see clearly and hear decisively from the Lord.

YOUR LEADERSHIP IS WORKING WHEN YOU ARE NOT WORKING IT

Once God begins to reveal to you His revelatory truths and to give you knowledge, His gift is working even when you are not working it. For instance, while preaching in the pulpit, many times my discernment kicks in without any warning. A young lady in the church can be sitting on one side of the room and a young man sitting on the other side. Unbeknownst to anyone else in the room, I can immediately discern their kindred spirits.

People often ask me how I can see in the spirit, cast out demons and operate in the gifts of the Spirit. There is no three-step program to teach spiritual warfare ministry. The answer is simple: Study the Word of God, seek His face and remain open to His voice of authority.

There are three major hindrances that stand between executing the Word of God with authority and operating in the gifts of the Spirit.

1. Wrong motives

Be truthful regarding your motive for ministry. Is it to win souls, set the captives free and meet the needs of the people? Or are you fascinated by the loaves and fishes? Are you awed by the miracles, signs and wonders to the point that you covet the gifts for self-glorification?

> And when Simon saw that through the laying on of the apostles' hands the Holy Spirit was given, he offered them money, saying, "Give me this power also, that anyone on whom I lay hands may receive the Holy Spirit." But Peter said to him, "Your money perish with you, because you thought that the gift of God could be purchased with money! You have neither part nor portion in this matter, for your heart is not right in the sight of God."
>
> —Acts 8:18–21

Many times we make the mistake of trying to acquire the gifts of God in the same way we acquire worldly assets—an impossible task. The gifts of God are not for sale, nor should they be for hire. Although it was fine for Simon to desire the gift, he tried to acquire it through the wrong means—with cash. Had Simon's heart been in the right place, he would have known that the gifts of God are nonnegotiable.

2. Lack of knowledge

I often see ministers with much zeal and no knowledge. In order to impart effectively into and impact a nation, you must be instant in season and out of season. I once asked a woman who held the title of *prophet* to prophecy over the ministry, to which she responded that her gift does not "work" like that, but that God turns it on and off at will.

I corrected her by going straight to the Word of God.

> Having then gifts differing according to the grace that is given to us, *let us use them:* if prophecy, *let us prophesy in proportion to our faith;* or ministry, let us use it in our ministry; he who teaches, in teaching.
> —ROMANS 12:6–7, EMPHASIS ADDED

We are told to prophesy "in proportion to our faith." Why? The Lord will honor the word of His prophets. That is why those who walk in the office of prophet or have a prophetic anointing upon their lives must be careful what they allow to be spoken out of their mouths. "My people are destroyed for lack of knowledge" (Hos. 4:6). Without knowledge, your ministry is doomed to failure even before it begins.

3. Being misplaced

In all your ways acknowledge Him,
And He shall direct your paths.

—PROVERBS 3:6

Understanding what you were created by God to accomplish is of utmost importance. Take time to acknowledge the Lord earnestly regarding every facet of your life, and He will direct your paths in the way that you should go. As you do, He will limit the disappointments that come to you as a result of man-made plans that only yield frustration.

Every person must find out what he or she was created to do and go forth in that area of ministry. In my case, God has given me the ability to see beyond the surface of natural things. In my spirit, those things have already taken place, although things may still look the same in the natural. I can often see things happening three or four weeks prior to their actual fulfillment. I honestly believe that my discernment level has a lot to do with not being too hasty to judge every situation and not being mean or evil toward others.

I realize that regardless of where others are in their spiritual walk with God, it is not my job to condemn, but to lead them to Christ. In whichever way He decides to use me, I have purposed to keep myself continually open to the voice of the Lord and to obey His will as He leads. God promises that when we place Him before our own personal desires, He will meet our need.

Therefore do not worry, saying, "What shall we eat?" or "What shall we drink?" or "What shall we wear?" For after all these things the Gentiles seek. For your heavenly Father knows that you need all these things. But seek first the kingdom of God and His righteousness, and all these things shall be added to you. Therefore do not worry about tomorrow, for tomorrow will worry about its own things.

—MATTHEW 6:31–34

Seek the righteousness of God, and know that He has not forgotten about the things that you have need of in your life. Never become too busy with the *work* of ministry that you forget the *Man* behind the ministry. Without Him your work becomes in vain. I rarely know, as it relates to specific times, when the Lord is going to use me to be a blessing to others.

Understanding what you were created by God to accomplish is of utmost importance.

From time to time God carries me through seasons of dreams. Even though I'm in that season, sometimes it takes me a few weeks to figure out that, indeed, I have entered that season of dreams. At certain times I will go through extended periods where I sleep through the night, and if I have a dream, I will have no recollection of what I dream. I simply dream, just like everyone else. If I am overworked, it interferes with my sleep life.

There are other times, however, when God speaks to

me about the direction of the church. There are seasons when He takes me to places that I have not yet visited but *will* visit in the future. I see people that I have not seen in a while, and by the following Sunday or Tuesday night, they are in church. Because of the way that the Lord deals with me, I have gained a great appreciation for being quiet...not allowing any interference into my spiritual life by speaking to someone who interprets dreams. I earnestly believe that the things God deposits into me during my sleep life will be revealed to me by Him in my awake life.

DEMONIC DREAMS AND REALISTIC MANIFESTATIONS

For four or five weeks before I went to minister in a large church in Atlanta, Georgia, I experienced demonic dreams at night. In the dreams I would be in crack houses where I saw people strung out on drugs. I saw disfigured animals and heard howling. In the dream, I was met by demonic figures as I walked up several stairwells.

In one dream I saw a person from our church who was walking around with a spirit of doubt resting upon her shoulder in the form of a talking bird. The bird spoke negative things to her, turning the truth into a lie and disguising his lying words as truth. In the natural, I never saw or realized this about her until after I had the dream. I had not realized that God gave me the dream as revelation about the season with which she was dealing. She had a great problem in discerning truth, which began to affect her job, relationships, family and so on. She was suspicious and didn't believe or trust anybody. It was due to that demonic bird that rested on her shoulders and whispered into her ears. So I prayed and asked God for revelation regarding this demonic bird that I had seen in my dream.

The Lord told me that the woman had a friend who lived in another city who would fly in and out several times a year. So that was the revelation about the bird aspect of the dream. The human link represented the demon that had lodged itself in the individual whom she had trusted. This woman's life would change completely, based on this other woman, a friend, who flew in and out.

When I spoke to that particular spirit, the girl manifested publicly in the church and was subsequently freed from the demon spirit. That same night she received a phone call from the friend out of town, who told her, "I don't think we're as close as we used to be. Why haven't you called me?"

We cast that spell off, but a few weeks later I saw her again and noticed that the spirit had come back. "Have you been talking to that person again?" I asked her.

Her answer was *yes*, and she explained to me that the strangest thing had occurred. She said that the night she was prayed for she went home, and the friend called her. "I don't understand," the woman told her, "What is the disconnect? I was just lying here, and I felt the need to call you. You don't like me anymore" . . . and so on.

I was able to get her to confess and renounce the spirit. Then I asked her if I could talk to the friend. The friend declined and wouldn't speak to me, but from that time forward, she also left the young lady alone.

I was faced with another situation as our church began to grow. Often I would lie awake in the middle of the night, dealing with my own personal issues and looking to the Lord for continual deliverance. Although I was able to stand before the people in the church and be the instrument of great blessing to them, the Lord was simultaneously revealing to me certain things that were going on in my own house—my own spiritual house.

I began to receive a series of light brushes on my face, as if a physical hand were touching me out of concern. The touches would move me to look in several directions. A touch at the top of my head would move my head downward, and another would move my cheek from side to side. In the Spirit, God was navigating my eyes to stroll throughout the congregation. One day he showed me a young lady in our church who had come to us from another ministry. I knew she was called there by God in order for me to nurture her—literally father her—so that she could be set free.

At the same time there was another young lady in our church who had been there for six years. I had been wrestling with her and her mind-set, and had already had several confrontational meetings with her about her need for deliverance from the spirit of rejection that warred against her. She was a gossiper, a semiworshiper and extremely jealous. She needed, lived for and desired acceptance at any price.

A triangle friendship had developed between this girl and two other young ladies in our church. The spirit of lesbianism was on these girls—not that they would engage in sexual behavior; however, the spirit was definitely there. The fourth component came in the form of the young lady from the other ministry.

As the Lord began to reveal more and more, the two

young ladies who had been in relationship with this girl eventually separated themselves from the manipulative union. At that point, the girl with whom I had been dealing for six years about her jealousy and need to control began to manifest an outward lesbian relationship with the young lady from the other ministry.

As I began to delve further into the situation, I realized that the only way to bring healing was to confront the parties involved. When the purpose of Satan is revealed, healing and deliverance have a way of taking over, soothing the pain that was inflicted upon the wounded vessel.

In speaking to these young ladies and confronting the situation, several lives were changed, deliverance took place, and healing was allowed to take its course.

God will always forewarn the spiritual leader of a church before a major occurrence happens that has the potential of seriously affecting or injuring the lives of those under his care. As believers, He also gives us the power to combat the forces of the enemy and covers us from being destroyed in the midst of the battle.

> Behold, I give you the authority to trample on serpents and scorpions, and over all the power of the enemy, and nothing shall by any means hurt you.
> —LUKE 10:19

Some time ago I was invited to preach at a conference. Upon concluding my message, an altar call was given, and people rushed the altar in an almost violent way as they were set free from the spirits of molestation, homosexuality, rejection, inferiority complexes and many diseases. During this altar call, which lasted for fifteen or twenty minutes, several demonic manifestations occurred as people were set free.

One young lady came up on the platform meowing like a cat. For nearly ten minutes we prayed and waited for God to give us revelation regarding her situation. She was wearing an ankle bracelet, and I was instructed through revelation from God to have her take the ankle bracelet off. When the ankle bracelet was removed, the girl was set free. Prior to removing the bracelet, she had shown outward manifestations of inward demonic possession, but after removing it she was set free from that manifestation and the demonic possessions that drove her.

> *God will always forewarn the spiritual leader of a church before a major occurrence happens that has the potential of seriously affecting or injuring the lives of those under his care.*

In our counseling session after the service, I asked her what was going on in her life. She shared with me that when she was nineteen, she had been involved in a lesbian relationship with a twenty-eight-year-old woman. Her lesbian lover had given her the ankle bracelet, and the meowing came out of their sexual encounters.

What I am sharing with you is shared through revelation. Regardless of how many myths you have been taught concerning religious and spiritual matters, I am a living witness that you will not be able to break or destroy curses without revelatory insight.

If you were not created or anointed by God in a certain area of ministry, you will never be able to develop the revelation or to train and excel in the level of deliverance needed to have victory in that particular ministry. Many people think that once they are filled with the Holy Spirit, they can do anything—but they cannot. They can only do what God has preordained them to do when the Holy Spirit empowers them. The Holy Spirit is the electricity—the charge—that gives power to the gift. The Holy Spirit is the power, the *dunamis,* the enablement, the electricity of the Spirit realm. He empowers you to do what you were created to do.

Don't allow the myths and lingo of religion to frustrate the cause of Christ that lies within you. Be careful also about allowing others to pull you into potholes of debates that seek to belittle the Word of God and to exalt the so-called knowledge of man.

Allowing the "word" of man to control your actions above and beyond the Word of God is a form of witchcraft. Anytime someone is able to bend your will and emotions toward his or her own will, that person has succeeded in pulling you into a manipulative web of witchcraft, which only furthers your bondage and scratches the itch that other person has for manipulation and control.

Ask the Lord to give you spiritual insight to enable you to dodge every stumbling block—every pothole of confusion—and to give you something you can understand for your own unique and personal situation. Break free from the manipulative setbacks of witchcraft and control. Hold on to the firm foundation of the Word of God. Arise and walk into the newness of a victorious life!

Wisdom is the principle thing; therefore get wisdom. And in all your getting, get understanding.

—PROVERBS 4:7

Six

Witchcraft for
the Common Man

Once the Lord has given you something that you can understand for your particular situation, it's very important to be wary of every snare of the enemy. He will use any cracked or open door to seduce you into a place where you don't belong. Satan knows that he can't take your gift, but he can cause you to compromise it to the point that it becomes questionable to unbelievers. There is great significance in the words of Proverbs 3:6: "In all your ways acknowledge Him, and He shall direct your paths." Early in ministry I learned the hard way just how unbelievably significant these "simple" instructions can be.

Once while I was in Haiti with a group of people, we were taken to a morgue filled with refrigerated compartments that held bodies on tables, each with a tag hanging from the feet. To our surprise, the undertaker told us that every person in that room was alive.

Witch doctors are so popular in Haiti that the religion of the nation is called *voodoo,* which is *witchcraft.* Voodoo witch doctors use drugs in some form to induce a deathlike state in their followers, and then use drugs to maintain them as "zombies"—the name given these bodies in the morgue. We were taken to this morgue because a Christian group of Haitians wanted us to go in to pray and break this spell.

But I was from America and had not yet been taught how to break demonic spells. The only thing I knew how to do was to preach—and I'm not even sure I had been taught how to do that properly. So there we stood inside that eerie place—where I didn't want to be in the first place. I was from New York City, and I wanted to go home! I didn't want to be in a room full of zombies. Are you kidding?

But as we walked into that dark, stench-reeking room, a Haitian man told us, "The last man we brought here to cast off the evil spirits of these people died." Then he asked us to call the evil spirits off these people.

I was thinking, *Hey! I am not the man for this job!* But there we were, so we started praying to the Father in the name of Jesus.

"Well, Lord..." we prayed as we looked around the room, "You said we shall lay hands on the sick, and they shall recover. You said we would raise those who are dead."

Suddenly, in the midst of our prayer, we heard a loud thud.

"Ooooh, Lord, let Your blood cover us," were the next words that came out of someone's mouth.

Nobody in the room got up—living or tagged. If they had, I would have been out of there in the blink of an eye! I wouldn't have needed a door either, because you would have seen my body shape in the wall! I knew we were under satanic influence, but I also knew that my training in America had not prepared me for this. So, needless to say, there was no breaking of that voodoo spell that day. But it did open my eyes to the need that existed there.

Most of us here in America have not seen that kind of demon possession. But when you visit Haiti, Africa or any number of other nations where witchcraft is a national phenomenon, you will get a fast lesson on Satan's manifested power.

Since that experience I have studied to show myself approved as a workman that does not need to be ashamed (2 Tim. 2:15). When in the presence of voodoo or the many forms of witchcraft that are practiced in the United States, the first step in dealing with the demonic is having spiritual knowledge of Satan's ways.

Many of the demonic strongholds that are prevalent in Haiti and other nations around the world are the result of very visible practices of voodoo and black magic, which have been passed down for many generations as a part of the culture. But in America, Satan is much more subtle.

THE CURE

Satan can be subtle, and we must always be on guard. The apostle Peter admonished us:

> Be sober, be vigilant; because your adversary the

113

devil walks about like a roaring lion, seeking whom he may devour. Resist him, steadfast in the faith, knowing that the same sufferings are experienced by your brotherhood in the world.

—1 PETER 5:8–9

Notice that Peter said the devil is "seeking whom he may devour." It does not say that he "devours whomever he seeks." The thing that makes the difference is your will.

The name of Jesus is fought against so strongly by Satan and his demons in the earth because "there is no other name under heaven given among men by which we must be saved" (Acts 4:12). Deliverance from Satan's power will always come to those who believe in the power of God's Word and in Jesus' name. When a person receives God's forgiveness through the name of Jesus Christ, the subtle lies of the enemy will be exposed.

When you take the name of Jesus and declare war on the enemy (spiritual warfare), there are no peace signings, no retreats, no standoffs. It is a battle to the death—winner takes all. The Bible says, "And from the days of John the Baptist until now the kingdom of heaven suffers violence, and the violent take it by force" (Matt. 11:12).

The full purpose for attending Bible school, Sunday school, prayer meetings and Bible studies should be to equip you as a member of God's church to do spiritual warfare—learning to wage war on the devil and possess what God has already given us. I certainly could have used such training before my experience with voodoo in Haiti. Since that time I have come to know and preach on the powerful truths of prophesying God's Word in every area of life to destroy the devil's works. *Prophesying* is proclaiming, decreeing, declaring and forth-telling the things God is going to do in determining your blessing. If it is written in the Word, it is your inheritance in life.

Deliverance from Satan's power will always come to those who believe in the power of God's Word and in Jesus' name.

In Galatians 3:13–14 we discover that any generational curse that has been passed down from generation to generation is broken through the blood of Christ.

> Christ has redeemed us from the curse of the law, having become a curse for us (for it is written, "Cursed is everyone who hangs on a tree"), that the blessing of Abraham might come upon the Gentiles in Christ Jesus, that we might receive the promise of the Spirit through faith.

This passage says that Jesus became a curse for us when He hung on the cross so that the Gentiles (all non-Jews) might obtain the blessings of the Lord. The devil may have assigned a territorial spirit, but Jesus became our sin sacrifice by allowing the sins of the world to be laid on His shoulders.

Because of this sacrifice, you could become the righteousness of God through Christ. He was wounded so that you could be healed. He took upon Himself all the sin of the world with you in mind, thinking that He would rather go to hell for you than to go to heaven without you.

Jesus knew you couldn't redeem yourself from the curse, so He became a curse for you in order to bless you. And when He did it, He looked down through ceaseless generations and saw the things that were going to plague your life.

In Galatians 5:19–21, Paul lists the works of the flesh:

> Now the works of the flesh are evident, which are: adultery, fornication, uncleanness, lewdness, idolatry, sorcery, hatred, contentions, jealousies, outbursts of wrath, selfish ambitions, dissensions, heresies, envy, murders, drunkenness, revelries, and the like.

Each of these is a work the devil is seeking daily to act out in people's lives—in your life. Some who choose to fulfill these lusts end up in prison, in witches' covens or dead. Others make them a regular part of their strife-filled lives and live in daily conflict with others around them in a cursed, miserable existence of spiritual and emotional pain.

A DWELLING PLACE

I believe that everyone on earth has been assigned a personal territorial demon that takes notes from day one of their lives. Some give these demons more room to express themselves than others, allowing them to build strongholds that control or possess their lives. To a certain degree, entire nations can be controlled when they have government-sponsored witchcraft. Haiti, with its voodoo religion involving sorcery and magic ritual, is a good example.

During my many travels, I often ask the question, "Where do demons come from?" Depending on the audience in attendance, I receive varying answers. Some believe they are the disembodied spirits of a pre-Adamic race that lived on the earth between Genesis 1:1 and Genesis 2:2. Others believe demons are fallen angels who were led astray in Lucifer's rebellion. But one thing is for sure—demons need a human body through which they can express themselves physically. They are constantly on the lookout for new "houses," as Jesus called them, through whom they can manifest.

> When an unclean spirit goes out of a man, he goes through dry places, seeking rest, and finds none. Then he says, "I will return to my house from which I came." And when he comes, he finds it empty, swept, and put in order. Then he goes and takes with him seven other spirits more wicked than himself, and they enter and dwell there; and the last state of that man is worse than the first. So shall it also be with this wicked generation.
>
> —MATTHEW 12:43–45

In this passage, Jesus pointed out that demons seek to dwell in human bodies and to control their actions. In Luke 5 Jesus delivered a man from such a condition. This man's actions were so controlled by the devils that possessed his body that he lived naked in a graveyard and continually cut himself with stones. (See Mark 5:5.)

> Then they sailed to the country of the Gadarenes, which is opposite Galilee. And when He stepped out on the land, there met Him a certain man

from the city who had demons for a long time. And he wore no clothes, nor did he live in a house but in the tombs. When he saw Jesus, he cried out, fell down before Him, and with a loud voice said, "What have I to do with You, Jesus, Son of the Most High God? I beg You, do not torment me!" For He had commanded the unclean spirit to come out of the man. For it had often seized him, and he was kept under guard, bound with chains and shackles; and he broke the bonds and was driven by the demon into the wilderness.

Jesus asked him, saying, "What is your name?"

And he said, "Legion," because many demons had entered him. And they begged Him that He would not command them to go out into the abyss.

Now a herd of many swine was feeding there on the mountain. So they begged Him that He would permit them to enter them. And He permitted them. Then the demons went out of the man and entered the swine, and the herd ran violently down the steep place into the lake and drowned.

—LUKE 8:26–33

In this Bible incident Jesus spoke to the devils. That doesn't mean, however, that ministering to the demonized should involve similar conversations with demonic beings. Jesus did this under the direction of the Holy Spirit. We also are not told the reason why He allowed the demons to possess the swine. Swine were unclean according to Old Testament Law, but there were unexplained reasons for His allowing their possession at the demons' request.

The point of this passage is this: This man was possessed by demons, and when Jesus commanded them to leave...*they had to go!* They implored the Lord not to send them into "the abyss" (v. 31). This abyss is the place where Satan will be imprisoned, as seen in Revelation 20:2.

This story in Luke illustrates the truth that certain people give their territorially assigned demons so much room to grow that eventually the demons are allowed to control and even possess the people's lives. This was certainly the case with the demoniac of the Gadarenes, as many have come to call him.

No Authority...No Control

However, much more common to the human experience in dealing with territorial spirits are the people who give these territorial spirits less authority, although they do submit to their control to a certain degree.

It is not necessary to turn control of our lives over to territorial spirits. It is very possible—and necessary—to sabotage their evil intentions for our lives. Even some people who do not know Christ have thwarted the devil's best efforts to ruin their lives. Why? Because the devil and his demons do not have authority and control in a person's life unless that person has been willing to submit to the devil's ideas—and some decide not to give in. The devil's control is limited to those people who give in when the enemy comes to persuade them.

There is a spirit behind what we call "peer pressure" that leads young people astray into unbridled passions, alcohol, drug abuse and, eventually, crime. But these young people don't have to submit. The will is always involved.

As a young boy growing up on the streets of New York City, I personally succumbed to Satan's lure into drug addiction. My desire to escape the oppressive conditions of my tough neighborhood overrode my desire to resist when offered the temporary escape of drugs. As a result, what began as a "one-time" experience of experimenting with drugs soon escalated into a $270-per-day cocaine habit. Drug abuse is a form of sorcery that manipulates the mind, confuses the thinking and further weakens the flesh. So strong was the addiction that I soon began to oppress others in order to satisfy my need. I robbed and stole whatever it took to quench the addiction and find relief.

> *The devil cannot make anyone do anything. He can only work to influence them.*

As I look back today, I can see that God gave His angels charge over me in order to get glory from my life. (See Psalm 91:11.) I did go to prison, but I found Christ there.

Today I stand as a living testimony that "if the Son makes you free, you shall be free indeed" (John 8:36). Although I owe to Him a debt that I can never fully repay, I gladly return unto Him my life and preach His Word all over the world, testifying of His liberating power and authority over every oppressive spirit, including addiction.

When you talk to men or women who end up in

prison, most of them have no idea of the role territorial demons had to play in their incarceration. That old Flip Wilson line, "The devil made me do it," had nothing to do with it, because the devil cannot make anyone do anything. He can only work to influence them.

Those who agree to move up to Satan's high place of promised power and authority do so because of their proven faith in his lies at the previous level. Before Nimrod agreed to build the Tower of Babel, he was convinced of the importance of the building project. (See Genesis 10:8–10; 11:1–9.) So he launched his campaign based on his belief. But he moved step by step in response to Satan's subtle recruitment because this is how the devil works—through a simple lie.

Those caught up in the witching craft end up basing their lives on witchcraft's rituals because they believed Satan's lies at different levels. Those people who are enslaved by the devil to his craft have opened their lives to full-blown demonic possession.

Others who deal with the reality of Satan's demons have no desire to step up to his next level or to be fully enmeshed in witchcraft. But, at the same time, because they do not have strong wills, the territorial demons seek to oppress them through suicide, sexual and substance addictions, unscrupulous business practices, shady politics and criminal behavior. By oppressing them with these bondages, the devil is able to keep people ignorant of spiritual truth, thus deceiving the very elect.

If the will of an individual allows that person to resist gospel truth, then the window has been opened to fulfilling Satan's plan. From that first level of resisting spiritual truth, the devil continually attempts to move that person to the next level, contributing even further to his devious will. His ultimate plan is to keep people caught up in deceit—his realm of authority.

FREEDOM THROUGH
THE POWER OF JESUS' NAME

Every curse the devil lays on you can be destroyed when the name of Jesus and His Word are applied on the basis of the cross. Those who have been drawn into witchcraft through the psychic hotlines are totally set free from their demonically invaded life through the power of Jesus' name.

Millions who are enslaved to Satan on varying levels of deception are set free and enter the liberty of God's Holy Spirit immediately through the power of Jesus' name.

All strongholds need the redeeming blood of Jesus and His Word to purify and destroy them.

But to be set free, you must do more than recognize that Satan is evil in all of his ways. You must also accept Jesus as your Lord and Savior. My core message to you in this book is my desire to dispel the myths that you may have been taught concerning religion and the spirit realm. I desire to give you a clearer understanding of your choices and rights through Jesus Christ.

When Jesus hung on the tree, He hung suspended between earth and glory until the sun went down—which initiated the "locking in" of the curse. But then He went down into the underworld and paid the price for our sins. Because He did, God has given us supernatural power and authority to speak out of our mouths against the curses of the devil. Not all curses are dissolved by the laying on of hands or the sprinkling of oil—many times they are destroyed by what we confess out of our mouths:

> But what does it say? "The word is near you, in your mouth and in your heart" (that is, the word of faith which we preach): that if you confess with your mouth the Lord Jesus and believe in your heart that God has raised Him from the dead, you will be saved.
>
> —ROMANS 10:8–9

As you will see in the next chapter, the sexual problems that plague many people date back through many generations—as do their bad teeth, cancer and alcoholism. Much of the baggage carried around by people today is the result of things that other people left as a legacy for them. Satan has laid claim to those conditions. Territorial demons simply hang around families and claim squatting rights.

In his realm of error, Satan is a legalist. So when he can enslave a person from birth, he will not only do so but also will presume some legal authority in doing it. Of course, God's authority outweighs his. But inherited influences passed down from one generation to another have always been a part of Satan's strategic plan. All strongholds, especially sensual ones that take root early in life, need the redeeming blood of Jesus and His Word to purify and destroy them. We must learn to view our deliverance as if we were on trial in a courtroom.

DESTROYING THE POWER OF WITCHCRAFT

Witchcraft and astrology have plagued the earth as long as Satan has walked on it. As Solomon said, there truly is nothing new under the sun (Eccles. 1:9). But because so few understand Satan's deceptions, there are always new revelations from God's Word to help others find their way.

In the Old Testament, God named and forbade witchcraft's well-established practices, which had plagued the nations since Nimrod's Tower of Babel project around 2200 B.C. New Testament apostles confronted witchcraft also. By examining closely God's Word on the matter in both the Old and New Testaments, you will recognize His instruction for utterly destroying the devil's witching craft.

> He who sins is of the devil, for the devil has sinned from the beginning. For this purpose the Son of God was manifested, that He might destroy the works of the devil.
>
> —1 JOHN 3:8

Every practice of witchcraft is an abomination unto God because it enslaves innocent people and slanders God's name. As we study the Old Testament, we find that every Hebrew patriarch was at least exposed to the practice. So, from the Bible's earliest texts we discover the mind of God on the matter.

Following Adam and Eve's fall from grace, Abraham became God's instrument for putting man back in contact with the true and living God. But it is apparent in Joshua 24:2 that Abraham himself once worshiped the gods of astrology:

> And Joshua said to all the people, "Thus says the
> LORD God of Israel: 'Your fathers, including
> Terah, the father of Abraham and the father of
> Nahor, dwelt on the other side of the River in old
> times; and they served other gods.'"
>
> —JOSHUA 24:2

It is also obvious in Exodus 32 that Abraham's seed learned about astrology and idol worship from the Egyptians during their 430-year captivity. In that chapter, we find the children of Israel making a golden calf to worship while Moses was on the mountain talking with God. Because of Israel's pagan involvement, God revealed His views about astrology in the following earliest passages of the Old Testament texts:

> You shall have no other gods before Me.
>
> —EXODUS 20:3

> When you come into the land which the LORD
> your God is giving you, you shall not learn to
> follow the abominations of those nations. There
> shall not be found among you anyone who makes
> his son or his daughter pass through the fire, or
> one who practices witchcraft, or a soothsayer, or
> one who interprets omens, or a sorcerer, or one
> who conjures spells, or a medium, or a spiritist, or
> one who calls up the dead. For all who do these
> things are an abomination to the LORD, and
> because of these abominations the LORD your
> God drives them out from before you.
>
> —DEUTERONOMY 18:9–12

> You shall not eat anything with the blood, nor
> shall you practice divination or soothsaying.
>
> —LEVITICUS 19:26

> And the person who turns to mediums and
> familiar spirits, to prostitute himself with them, I
> will set My face against that person and cut him
> off from his people.
>
> —LEVITICUS 20:6

These earliest passages of Scripture reveal God's views on Satan worship. As you study the Scriptures closely, you also see how God's power has been resident throughout history to destroy Satan's witching craft.

MOSES VS. PHARAOH

When Moses took on Pharaoh's astrologers and magicians, the power of God humiliated them and their dark master in utter defeat.

> So Moses and Aaron went in to Pharaoh, and
> they did so, just as the LORD commanded. And
> Aaron cast down his rod before Pharaoh and
> before his servants, and it became a serpent. But
> Pharaoh also called the wise men and the sor-
> cerers; so the magicians of Egypt, they also did
> in like manner with their enchantments. For
> every man threw down his rod, and they became
> serpents. But Aaron's rod swallowed up their
> rods.
>
> —EXODUS 7:10–12

When Satan's spirit of rebellion challenged God's established authority, God sent fire from heaven to consume some of Satan's followers and to swallow up the rest in the earth:

> So they and all those with them went down alive into the pit; the earth closed over them, and they perished from among the assembly. Then all Israel who were around them fled at their cry, for they said, "Lest the earth swallow us up also!" And a fire came out from the LORD and consumed the two hundred and fifty men who were offering incense.
>
> —NUMBERS 16:33−35

ELIJAH VS. BAAL

When Elijah confronted the prophets of Baal, God sent fire from heaven to destroy Baal worship in Israel, and then empowered His prophet to kill 450 men.

> Then the fire of the LORD fell and consumed the burnt sacrifice, and the wood and the stones and the dust, and it licked up the water that was in the trench. Now when all the people saw it, they fell on their faces; and they said, "The LORD, He is God! The LORD, He is God!" And Elijah said to them, "Seize the prophets of Baal! Do not let one of them escape!" So they seized them; and Elijah brought them down to the Brook Kishon and executed them there.
>
> —1 KINGS 18:38−40

THE HEBREW CHILDREN VS. NEBUCHADNEZZAR'S COURT

When Daniel, along with the other Hebrew children, was inducted into Nebuchadnezzar's court, God demonstrated to the king that His power was ten times greater than the power of Satan:

> Then the king interviewed them, and among them all none was found like Daniel, Hananiah, Mishael, and Azariah; therefore they served before the king. And in all matters of wisdom and understanding about which the king examined them, he found them ten times better than all the magicians and astrologers who were in all his realm.
>
> —DANIEL 1:19–20

In each of these biblical examples, God belittled and destroyed Satan's powers of astrology to show His superiority over Satan's works in the earth. Therefore, how much more should we, as God's New Testament church, be assured of our spiritual power over modern witchcraft in the earth?

But do we really exercise our spiritual power over the occult? I don't think we do. If we did, every psychic hotline would be out of business, and everyone in witches' covens would either turn to the Lord or live in dread of God's powerful local church.

The spiritual warfare rights and the power of attorney we have received in Jesus' name will destroy the devil's works. But they must be applied in faith to release God's superior power into our daily fight.

Now, I know that there aren't very many of us who are "there"—walking in that place of proper spiritual authority. So please don't take my last few statements in a condemning way. Rather, take them as an opportunity to grow in faith. As we complete this book by looking at the delivering power of God's Holy Spirit, which was released in His earliest church, I believe it will inspire and equip us, by faith, to destroy Satan's work by releasing that same delivering power of God today.

PHILIP, PETER AND JOHN VS. SIMON

Witchcraft was a huge cultural phenomenon in the earliest days of the church, as recorded in the Book of Acts. When the church was "scattered throughout the regions of Judea and Samaria," the evangelist Philip started a crusade in the city of Samaria (Acts 8:1, 5).

Samaria was the city where the wicked queen Jezebel instituted Baal worship in Israel. (See 1 Kings 16:24–32.) Nine hundred years before Philip brought the gospel into the city, Elijah destroyed her prophets and mocked Satan's worship. But by the time Philip arrived, Satan's witchcraft had taken root again, and many of Samaria's inhabitants were under curses or spells. It was also in Samaria that Simon the sorcerer had taken control of this city through his magic powers. That is, until Philip, then Peter and John, arrived in Samaria.

> Then Philip went down to the city of Samaria and preached Christ to them. And the multitudes with one accord heeded the things spoken by Philip, hearing and seeing the miracles which he did.
> —ACTS 8:5–6

Many of Samaria's people were in the captivity of demons. So the first thing Philip let them know was that Jesus came to set them free. He may have preached from Isaiah 61:1: "The LORD has...sent Me to heal the brokenhearted, to proclaim liberty to the captives." But

Philip didn't just come to show them God's reality—he came to help them experience it. The result?

> For unclean spirits, crying with a loud voice, came out of many who were possessed; and many who were paralyzed and lame were healed.
>
> —ACTS 8:7

The gospel lifts people with the knowledge that Jesus came to give to man God's abundant life. But, at the same time, it reveals the truth that Satan comes to steal, kill and destroy people's lives (John 10:10).

As we study God's Word, we can discern the charlatans from God's true messengers.

After the Spirit of God delivered many from demon possession and physical sickness, Satan's head astrologer in Samaria, Simon the sorcerer, came to find out about this power that was greater than his:

> But there was a certain man called Simon, who previously practiced sorcery in the city and astonished the people of Samaria, claiming that he was someone great.
>
> —ACTS 8:9

Simon, like so many psychics parading around American TV airwaves today, put on an air of spirituality. And since the people were ignorant of the true and living God, they didn't understand the source of Simon's power. So they feared him.

...to whom they all gave heed, from the least to the greatest, saying, "This man is the great power of God." And they heeded him because he had astonished them with his sorceries for a long time.

—ACTS 8:10–11

SIMON LIVES

Things haven't changed. There are many Simons among us today who are accepted and revered as representatives of God. But as we study God's Word, we can discern the charlatans from God's true messengers. The charlatans use bondage and control, which have become too common in the church today, and often "charge" to pray for the sick. A word to the wise is sufficient.

When Simon saw the demonstration of God's power and heard the gospel, he believed and was baptized. Then when Peter and John went down from Jerusalem to minister the baptism of the Holy Spirit to Samaria's converts, Simon tried to buy God's power. But when he did, Peter rebuked Simon for his gall and iniquity, driving the new convert to his knees, saying, "Pray to the Lord for me, that none of the things which you have spoken may come upon me" (Acts 8:24).

PAUL VS. ELYMAS

When Elymas the sorcerer opposed Paul on the island of Paphos, the Spirit of God struck the sorcerer blind.

Now when they had gone through the island to Paphos, they found a certain sorcerer, a false prophet, a Jew whose name was Bar-Jesus, who was with the proconsul, Sergius Paulus, an intelligent man. This man called for Barnabas and Saul and sought to hear the word of God. But Elymas the sorcerer (for so his name is translated) withstood them, seeking to turn the proconsul away from the faith. Then Saul, who also is called Paul, filled with the Holy Spirit, looked intently at him and said, "O full of all deceit and all fraud, you son of the devil, you enemy of all righteousness, will you not cease perverting the straight ways of the Lord? And now, indeed, the hand of the Lord is upon you, and you shall be blind, not seeing the sun for a time."

And immediately a dark mist fell on him, and he went around seeking someone to lead him by the hand. Then the proconsul believed, when he saw what had been done, being astonished at the teaching of the Lord.

—Acts 13:6–12

Paul was doing God's will when he encountered this practitioner of witchcraft, and the Holy Spirit empowered Paul's words. Never forget that! Never forget the power of your confession when it is rooted in God's sovereign will. Sergius Paulus, the island's governor, repented of his sin as he witnessed this power of God.

PAUL AND SILAS VS. THE CRAFT

When Paul and Silas ministered in Philippi, they met a woman possessed with a spirit of divination. Remember, divination is the practice of using the stars and evil spirits to foretell the future.

Now it happened, as we went to prayer, that a certain slave girl possessed with a spirit of divination met us, who brought her masters much profit by

132

> fortune-telling. This girl followed Paul and us, and
> cried out, saying, "These men are the servants of
> the Most High God, who proclaim to us the way
> of salvation." And this she did for many days.
>
> But Paul, greatly annoyed, turned and said to
> the spirit, "I command you in the name of Jesus
> Christ to come out of her." And he came out that
> very hour. But when her masters saw that their
> hope of profit was gone, they seized Paul and
> Silas and dragged them into the marketplace to
> the authorities.
>
> —ACTS 16:16–19

This fortuneteller, as we would call her today, worked for a group of men who marketed her services. But when Paul recognized her true mission in dogging his tracks, he cast the evil spirits from her so she could no longer cast spells. How? By exercising the gift of the discerning of spirits, as mentioned in 1 Corinthians 12:10, and the power of Jesus' name. When he detected the woman's demonic disturbance, he declared, "I command you in the name of Jesus Christ to come out of her." And the woman was free.

These kinds of demonic disturbances aren't all that uncommon in many churches today. When leaders aren't sensitive to the Holy Spirit, Satan's agents can destroy their ability to step out on God's Word. But if we are led by the Spirit of God, we can bind and cast these spirits out, as Paul did—in Jesus' name!

PAUL VS. THE BOOK OF SHADOWS

When Paul entered the city of Ephesus, the ministry of

the Holy Spirit was so powerful in destroying the strongholds of witchcraft that "many of those who had practiced magic brought their books together and burned them in the sight of all" (Acts 19:19).

In Ephesus the witch doctors of Paul's day realized that the power Paul demonstrated was greater than anything they had ever seen. They noticed he didn't use potions, charm bags or sacrifices, and they were stunned by the authority of Jesus' name. As a result, a group of seven local men attempted to cast out demons by imitating what Paul did—and they were beaten bloody for their efforts.

> Then some of the itinerant Jewish exorcists took it upon themselves to call the name of the Lord Jesus over those who had evil spirits, saying, "We exorcise you by the Jesus whom Paul preaches." Also there were seven sons of Sceva, a Jewish chief priest, who did so.
>
> And the evil spirit answered and said, "Jesus I know, and Paul I know; but who are you?"
>
> Then the man in whom the evil spirit was leaped on them, overpowered them, and prevailed against them, so that they fled out of that house naked and wounded. This became known both to all Jews and Greeks dwelling in Ephesus; and fear fell on them all, and the name of the Lord Jesus was magnified.
>
> —ACTS 19:13–17

It appears that the demonic possession of this man in Ephesus gave him strength similar to that of the demoniac of the Gadarenes, which I discussed earlier in this chapter. This demon-possessed man beat these seven sons of Sceva until they were bloody and naked because they obviously had no authority to use the name of Jesus. They weren't born again and didn't know God's power, so they used the name of Paul—"We exorcise you by the Jesus whom Paul preaches"—with horrible results.

Until we accept the Lord Jesus into our hearts, we aren't part of God's kingdom. This was the bad news for Sceva's sons. But it is good news for every one of us who have received the grace and power of the Holy Spirit and who have inherited the right to use Jesus' name.

So again the apostle Paul, as well as Luke and Mark, teaches us to confront and destroy the power of witchcraft through faith in Jesus' name.

> Behold, I give you the authority to trample on serpents and scorpions, and over all the power of the enemy, and nothing shall by any means hurt you.
>
> —LUKE 10:19

> And these signs will follow those who believe: In My name they will cast out demons; they will speak with new tongues.
>
> —MARK 16:17

A look at the result of Paul's Ephesus ministry proves again the superiority of God's power over the deceptions of witchcraft when a believer walks in New Testament faith.

> And many who had believed came confessing and telling their deeds. Also, many of those who had

practiced magic brought their books together
and burned them in the sight of all. And they
counted up the value of them, and it totaled fifty
thousand pieces of silver. So the word of the Lord
grew mightily and prevailed.

—ACTS 19:18–20

The books that were burned in the town square at
Ephesus probably included their *Book of Shadows.*
This was a book of witchcraft that contained everything Satan's followers had learned about sorcery and
magic over the previous twenty-three hundred years.
This was Ephesus's way of saying that God's power
and the name of Jesus were greater than anything Satan
had to offer.

HELL'S RESPONSE

These accounts in the Book of Acts not only show us
the power God has invested in His church, but also they
destroy Satan's works. They give us a look at what
happens when the demonic hosts of witchcraft are confronted by the power of God. When Satan's enterprises
are destroyed by God's power, Satan always persecutes
the vessels who release God's power.

Paul and Silas were thrown into jail after delivering
the woman in Philippi. When Peter released the Holy
Spirit's signs and wonders in Acts 5, he was persecuted
by a religious group known as the Sadducees.

Stephen preached against the astrology behind
Israel's idolatry in Acts 7, and he was stoned to death.

And they made a calf in those days, offered sacrifices to the idol, and rejoiced in the works of their

own hands. Then God turned and gave them up to worship the host of heaven, as it is written in the book of the Prophets: "Did you offer Me slaughtered animals and sacrifices during forty years in the wilderness, O house of Israel?" ...

When they heard these things they were cut to the heart, and they gnashed at him with their teeth ... Then they cried out with a loud voice, stopped their ears, and ran at him with one accord; and they cast him out of the city and stoned him. And the witnesses laid down their clothes at the feet of a young man named Saul.

–ACTS 7:41–42, 54, 57–58

Following their tremendous success in Ephesus, Paul and Silas were eventually forced to leave because an idol-maker named Demetrius stirred up the business community.

For a certain man named Demetrius, a silversmith, who made silver shrines of Diana, brought no small profit to the craftsmen. He called them together with the workers of similar occupation, and said: "Men, you know that we have our prosperity by this trade. Moreover you see and hear that not only at Ephesus, but throughout almost all Asia, this Paul has persuaded and turned away many people, saying that they are not gods which are made with hands. So not only is this trade of ours in danger of falling into disrepute, but also the temple of the great goddess Diana may be despised and her magnificence destroyed, whom all Asia and the world worship."

Now when they heard this, they were full of
wrath and cried out, saying, "Great is Diana of
the Ephesians!" So the whole city was filled with
confusion, and rushed into the theater with one
accord, having seized Gaius and Aristarchus,
Macedonians, Paul's travel companions. And
when Paul wanted to go in to the people, the disciples would not allow him. Then some of the
officials of Asia, who were his friends, sent to him
pleading that he would not venture into the theater... After the uproar had ceased, Paul called
the disciples to himself, embraced them, and
departed to go to Macedonia.
                              —ACTS 19:24–31; 20:1

From these examples, we can understand why many
preachers don't preach against witchcraft, cast out
devils or lay hands on the sick in America today.
"Those things only happened in the Bible days," they
tell their congregations, "and miracles aren't for
today." These are doctrines of the devil, which he continues to use today in his evil quest to enslave more
people.

And while many churches seem happy to build bigger
buildings and send missionaries thousands of miles
away, the witching craft in America is growing larger
and more popular every day.

The world is falling prey to Satan's witchcraft via
psychic hotlines every hour. Our movies and television
programs continue to serve as Satan's subtle pulpits of
deceit. Many of God's beloved saints are bound in
demonic deception, and they ignorantly accept it. But

Jesus died to destroy these works. So what are you going to do?

IT'S TIME TO ACT

To those of you who have fallen prey to Satan's doctrines of deceit and have abandoned the battle, I say: It is time to *act* on the Word of God. It is time to learn how to pray.

The Book of Acts is called the Acts of the Apostles, and now is the time for us to follow suit. Satan may work through human beings to come against us, but if that happens, we must stand on God's Word, which says, "No weapon formed against you shall prosper" (Isa. 54:17).

> *It is time to act on the*
> *Word of God. It is time to learn*
> *how to pray.*

Like the apostles, we as Christians have the same gift and ability—through Christ—to cast out devils and destroy Satan's works. (See Acts 1:8.) But again, we must believe it and go to work.

As saints of the Most High God, we should know that the hand of God is always with us. We must allow our prayers to ascend into heaven as incense every day. And we should pray for, support and exhort others who stand up against Satan and his demonic kingdom.

Remember, Satan works under the cover of darkness through deceptive disguises and fairytale facades. His crafty works are meant to enslave men's souls in shadowy, subtle ways. This is why Paul wrote, "But all things that are exposed are made manifest by the light, for whatever makes manifest is light" (Eph. 5:13).

Strike a match in a dark room, and light will overpower the darkness. Likewise, let us preach truth in our churches, over our airwaves and in the streets. When Satan's witchcraft appears in our culture, let us call God's angels into the fight to establish His ways. Let us awake from our neglect and shout out the deceit of Satan's subtle ways. The power of Christ will destroy Nimrod's new towers, but we—His born-again church— must light the way with the fullness of God's Spirit and the brightness of His truth. No matter how touchy a subject might be, if it's a great hindrance in the church, it must be addressed.

Keep your heart with all diligence,
for out of it spring the issues of life.

————————

—PROVERBS 4:23

Seven

Cancerous Sex

The enemy uses another form of witchcraft to divert Christians from God's plan. Satan often tries to twist a person's will to pursue fleshly pleasure through sexual intimacy. Sex has long been used to fill the void in the lives of both men and women. While women have been known to give sex to acquire love, men tend to profess love to acquire sex. All too often, the two objectives collide, collapsing the imaginary bridge that brought the couple together as one.

Sexuality, though given by God for the sole purpose of pleasure within the covenant bonds of marriage and for the reproduction of life, can also carry a very strong oppressive and destructive spirit when misused or abused. If you don't think sexual temptation has been used by Satan to destroy the work of God over the last two decades, you haven't read many newspapers or watched television. We all possess the emotions of sexuality within, which is why certain disciplines must be maintained in order to refrain from falling prey to our weaknesses in this area. Perhaps even more dangerous than the actual weakness is denying that these feelings exist.

> Flee sexual immorality. Every sin that a man does is outside the body, but he who commits sexual immorality sins against his own body.
> —1 CORINTHIANS 6:18

The aftereffects of immoral sexual behavior become the means of enslaving many to addictive behavior. Those who engage in unbridled sexual acts can become heirs to various transmitted spirits and strongholds in life. When this form of oppression takes root, healing becomes necessary. Along with a daily intake of the Word of God during the healing process, a person must also practice the discipline of abstaining to ensure the strength of the spiritual immune system.

Sexuality can carry a very strong oppressive and destructive spirit when misused or abused.

To better understand the impact of sexual sins on spiritually transmitted illnesses that invade people to deceive them, let's first examine the consequences of sexual sins of the natural.

STDs—SEXUALLY TRANSMITTED DISEASES

In today's promiscuous society, when two individuals come together in physical intimacy, they risk illness from the transference of bodily fluids. Sexually transmitted diseases (STDs) are, alarmingly, quite common. In the United States alone, more than sixty-five million people have an incurable STD, with an additional fifteen million becoming infected each year.[1]

STDs—Spiritually Transferred Demons

But untracked, and unknown to most, are the spiritually transmitted diseases, deceptions and spirits connected with sex. As it is in the natural, so it is in the spiritual. When an unlawful sexual connection is made, it always comes at a cost.

Many times in forbidden relationships a person finds himself struggling to refrain from continuing to have sex with the person with whom he has been intimate. This is because when a man and woman join their flesh, they not only experience moments of physical pleasure, but they also inherit a part of the other individual's spirit.

The tempting lie that "one time won't hurt" has forced many great men and women of God to their knees begging and pleading with God to deliver them from a destructive lifestyle that seems to have no end. Sexual addictions can be as dangerous and alluring as drug addiction. And as surprising as it may seem, there are people today in the church who are suffering silently from this painful truth.

A number of ungodly spirits can be transferred through the bond of sexual intimacy, including greed, lust for power and wealth, and unfaithfulness, just to name a few. The spirit of sexual oppression will attempt to deceive you into thinking you will walk away the same person you were before the act was committed. But this simply isn't true.

> Can a man take fire to his bosom,
> And his clothes not be burned?
> Can one walk on hot coals,
> And his feet not be seared?
> So is he who goes in to his neighbor's wife;
> Whoever touches her shall not be innocent.
> —PROVERBS 6:27–29

Both parties involved in an illicit sexual encounter will always walk away having acquired spirits that were once nonexistent, whether good or bad.

A PRESCRIPTION FOR PAIN

The following scenario unfolds daily in the lives of many women. After divorcing her husband, Abby was left with an unbearable pain that seemed to torture her continually with no relief in sight. It was the first thing she thought about in the morning and the last thing on her mind before she fell asleep at night. She swore she would never love again, trust again and especially be fooled again into an imaginary relationship based on piles of empty promises. She threw herself into her work, studying the Word of God and praying daily.

Although the pain had not fully subsided, she did find comfort and relief. *Finally,* Abby thought, *I'm on my way to a new beginning. I can breathe again and prepare for a fresh, new start.* The pain had begun to subside, and Abby graciously invited healing to repair the wounds of her heart.

Then she met Jason. Through a mutual friend, Abby

146

and Jason met one day at a family gathering. He was everything Abby wanted, but also everything she shouldn't have. Jason was assertive, goal-oriented, self-motivated and driven to pursue whatever he desired. Jason, however, was not saved and showed no signs of looking for any type of romantic commitment. It didn't take Abby long to weigh her options before deciding that Jason was trouble. Still, she thought that exchanging phone numbers would be fine; perhaps they could just be friends. With numbers exchanged, they both went on their way.

Abby found herself rushing to the phone every time it rang—wishing, hoping, "Maybe it's Jason calling to ask me out"—until one day the phone rang, and it was Jason. She took a deep breath and without hesitation gladly accepted his invitation. As the story goes, Abby eventually became engulfed in Jason's world, and the fact that she eventually sealed this bond by having sex with him only tightened the knot. Before she even realized how deeply she had allowed herself to fall, Abby found herself rushing to the phone for Jason's call, daydreaming about him constantly and dropping everything at a moment's notice to meet him and his demands. His likes became her likes; his goals, her goals; his appetites, her appetites.

Eventually, however, the phone stopped ringing, and Jason began to ignore her calls. Abby demanded an answer.

"What went wrong?" she questioned Jason.

"Well, I was beginning to feel that you were ready for a relationship, and I'm just not ready for that right now, so I thought it best for me to just back off," Jason explained.

Abby was crushed. She felt as if, again, her world was shattered. "How could I have been so stupid?" she chastised herself. "I saw this coming, and yet I still walked right into it."

Abby had no choice but to admit that if she was ever going to truly be set free, she had to face unresolved issues and stop medicating the pain and ignoring the illness that caused it. She realized that for years it had been easier for her to seek temporal relief rather than face the root cause of her problems. Allowing men to fill the void in her life became her self-prescribed comfort for many of the unresolved issues that haunted her daily. Abby finally realized that if she was ever going to be successful in life, she had to break away from the lie and embrace the truth. She was suffering from very cancerous toxins of emotional and mental anguish that dated back to her childhood.

Though Abby hated the way her father managed his home and how he treated her and the rest of the family, she often found herself choosing men who acted just like him. She embraced them wholeheartedly and would do whatever it took to please them, even if it meant sacrificing her own needs. If this cancerous seed of rejection was ever going to be healed, she knew she had to allow herself to go through the process of self-awareness and confrontation—the long-overdue chemotherapy she needed to kill this spiritual cancer residing in her mental and emotional anatomy.

It would be a painful process, but Abby understood the seriousness of her situation. Many women, and sometimes men, find themselves in this same predicament. They allow the mental and emotional illnesses of their pasts to incubate, while self-medicating the pain with the temporal relief of sex and relationship fantasies. Abby allowed herself to become consumed with Jason, and through sexual contact she became one with him. When you have sexual contact with a person, you not only have physical contact, but you unknowingly leave with a part of that person's spirit as well.

INCUBATED DANGER

Medically speaking, the time between infection and the physical appearance of infection is called the incubation period. The average incubation period for the sexually transmitted disease syphilis is twenty-one days.[2] This means that within this twenty-one-day time frame, no precautions are being taken to ensure the safety of the other individual. Neither is the infected person receiving proper medical care. Syphilis is silently growing and coming to fruition.

Satan's greatest weapon is to plant the seed of sin in our hearts. Then he waits patiently for the incubation period to take place.

Even after the physical manifestation of syphilis surfaces, which appears as a painless sore, this physical evidence heals itself in one to five weeks. But that doesn't mean the disease has gone into remission. In fact, when the actual sore disappears, it gives a false hope of healing because the syphilis infection is still very much a reality.[3]

Spiritually speaking, the same deceptive external realities exist in the transference of sexual spirits. Satan's greatest weapon is to plant the seed of sin in our hearts. Then he waits patiently for the incubation period to take place. He deceives his victims by producing the illusion of perfect health—when, in fact, Satan's specialized spirits are just waiting for the right time to surface.

"Unrepentant repentance" will eventually produce a reprobate mind.

Physical evidence of illness will follow an encounter, but within a few weeks, it may appear to be nonexistent. Spiritually, this is Satan's way of deceiving an individual into thinking he is fine. At first, sexual partners may feel some strain and guilt—the result of the voice of their conscience. Then as time passes, they may feel relieved. What they don't understand is that the spiritual and physical immune systems of those who fall into sexual sin will be challenged or even destroyed. The hot coals spoken of in Proverbs 6:27–28 may grow dim for a while, but they don't burn out.

SEXUAL STRONGHOLDS

When a sexual stronghold has been created, it takes more than prayer to bring forth deliverance. The habits in your lifestyle must be changed, and the need to abstain from fleshly desires is an absolute must. Whatever the source of the stronghold, it must become the target of attack if the stronghold is to be broken. Ignorance in this area only further handicaps and enslaves anyone who honestly desires to be set free.

In Abby's case, where sexual intimacy created a soul tie, the only way she could break this addictive spirit was through prayer and fasting, and abstaining from further sexual encounters. But before any of this could become reality, she had to desire to be set free. As was true in Abby's case, honesty with yourself and God is a definite must because only then can true repentance spring forth. You should never repent for something that you have no intention of releasing. "Unrepentant repentance" will eventually produce a reprobate mind, endangering the one so deluded with a continual life of sin.

PERVERSION AND PROMISCUITY

Two of the most common problems that can develop from sexually transmitted spirits are perversion and promiscuity. The soul tie formed through the bondage of promiscuity is, in most cases, extraordinarily hard to break. This is because the soul of the promiscuous individual is scattered among a host of mates, all of whom have contributed their own individual oppressive spirits into this one person. Women especially, because of their sensitive emotional makeup, find that soul ties birthed out of promiscuity are extremely binding. As a result, they, more than men, find themselves habitually falling into the clutches of ex-mates and sex partners whom they declared they would never see again. Again, all of this can result from soul ties that were specifically formed out of lust. They work to keep the one in bondage enslaved to a life of constant instability.

Do you not know that he who is joined to a harlot
is one body with her? For "the two," He says,
"shall become one flesh."

—1 CORINTHIANS 6:16

Men are not exempt from this kind of bondage to
promiscuity. The soul ties some men have to previous
partners can be so strong they mentally relive sex acts
they had with former mates. So the destructive results of
promiscuity in both women and men can continually risk
their well-being, causing them to be drawn to previous
partners—long after the relationships have been severed.

THE SEXUALLY TRANSFERRED DEMON OF HOMOSEXUALITY

Another destructive soul tie that can be sexually transmitted is homosexuality. Many cases of homosexuality
are transmitted through past sexual molestation that
occurred during childhood. When this sort of perverted
violation occurs, not only is a child's innocence ripped
away, but also, unbeknownst to the child, the will to be
set free is also taken.

So strong are these oppressive ties that few are able
to find deliverance and freedom from this slave-
binding, ongoing struggle. In addition to prayer, the
person deceived and oppressed by this spirit must
engage in consistent godly counsel. They especially
need to be encouraged to reject former sexual habits
while establishing new behaviors.

Those struggling with homosexuality often live in
denial, which must be addressed before they can experience deliverance. In order to be set free, the individual

must first identify and acknowledge that the problem exists. The greatest weapon against Satan's arsenal of deception is information and confrontation. But many times, even as parents, we tend to cover up the real issues. We sometimes deceive ourselves into thinking our child will grow out of it, and by doing so we give free rein to the enemy.

Anytime there are past occurrences of sexual perversion or promiscuity within a family, the maturing of these traits can manifest in future generations. Children will sometimes unknowingly act out the lifestyles of their relatives as the latest transmitters of their family's generational curses. If you ever happen to be put in a position to minister to such a child, the spirit that is in operation must be denounced through the blood of Jesus if deliverance is to take place. Of course, always remember to use wisdom so you do not frighten the child, who in most cases is totally oblivious to what is happening.

There must always be balance and consistency when dealing with this kind of abuse.

ALEX'S STORY

Because of the shame Alex endured through molestation, he never confronted the new attraction to men he had been feeling. His mother saw these traits developing, but she thought he was just going through a phase and would eventually grow out of it. However, by the time Alex reached adulthood, his mother was finally praying for freedom from his condition.

Alex the adult saw no need to seek the freedom his mother now desired for him, so he continued his promiscuous homosexual behavior. Alex was set free by the power of God for a brief period, but because he didn't exercise discipline and seek consistent godly counsel, he soon fell back into his old lifestyle. This time, however, Alex was visited by seven stronger demons, and he became even more lawless in his perversion. This soul tie had become a yoke around his neck that was much too heavy for him to manage.

After years of wandering, Alex finally returned to the fellowship of the church. Nonetheless, he still struggles with the curse of this aggressive spirit. His family, however, continues to pray that the Lord will deliver Alex so he may enjoy the liberty of a true relationship with Christ. Alex's story serves as a sobering reminder of the importance of staying free once set free by the power of God. Studying the Bible, spending time in prayer and attending a church that provides good spiritual food are musts if you are going to maintain victory and avoid the many struggles of sexual addiction.

Untying the Knots That Bind

In order to undo the damage of a soul tie, a spiritual untying must take place. The power of loosing and binding must be exercised.

> And I will give you the keys of the kingdom of heaven, and whatever you bind on earth will be bound in heaven, and whatever you loose on earth will be loosed in heaven.
>
> —Matthew 16:19

Knots that have been illegally formed in your life do not

have the authority to reign. Bondage to soul ties should be considered as life-or-death situations and be viewed with the severity Paul described in 1 Corinthians 6:9–10.

> Do you not know that the unrighteous will not inherit the kingdom of God? Do not be deceived. Neither fornicators, nor idolaters, nor adulterers, nor homosexuals, nor sodomites, nor thieves, nor covetous, nor drunkards, nor revilers, nor extortioners will inherit the kingdom of God.

None of us can afford to be sexually deceived. Satan's oppressive spirit of sexual destruction is at work in the church today. Can you think of a minister— famous or not—who shipwrecked his ministry because he gave in to the lust of the flesh? Have you heard of any Christian divorce cases that were the result of infidelity? You probably have.

No cry is too meaningless for Him to soothe, and no sin is too great for Him to forgive.

The enemy uses his sexually transmitted spirits and deceptions to destroy the ministry God has predestined for each individual. Satan knows that the seed God has planted within His people will grow into maturity to touch the lives of many others. So he subtly uses sexual temptations to distract God's people, get them off course and keep them away from the things God has for them. He lures those he can—to the point of death if they allow it. But praise God for those who have their mind and vision firmly planted in God's Word. Satan can't deceive these folks, so he will have to look elsewhere to create his next sexual deviant!

If you have been snared through the power of illicit sex or are being tempted now to become involved in it, I tell you the same thing Paul said in 1 Corinthians 6:18—run! Run to God for clarity of mind; His Word will show you what the deceptive encounter will eventually produce—hot coals, misery and possibly death.

God never repents for the gift He places within us, but He allows His mercy to rest upon us. No cry is too meaningless for Him to soothe, and no sin is too great for Him to forgive. You can be set free from sexual sins by His power and anointing. So if you have been dealing with this type of oppressive sexual attack, earnestly seek the Lord in your private time, and ask Him to guide you to freedom.

As you continue to pray and study the Word of God, may His grace and mercy be upon you, giving you the strength you need to ensure your change of lifestyle and to maintain your newfound freedom and to walk in victory. Study 1 Corinthians 6 very closely—then be sensitive to God's Spirit concerning what to do next.

And we know that all things work together for good to those who love God, to those who are the called according to His purpose.

—ROMANS 8:28

Eight

Oppression—Loosing the Tie That Binds

In the previous chapter we discussed the oppressive spirits that ungodly sexual contact can invite into a person's life. We saw how Satan turns what was meant to be a blessing into a curse. Religion teaches that "real" Christians are incapable of being oppressed and that all a believer needs to do is to get saved.

Although all things work together for the "good," a believer must do his part to maintain a healthy and meaningful relationship with Christ and be able to discern spiritual matters. The devil's ultimate goal is to get us to suppress our weaknesses rather than confront them and ask God for guidance. If he succeeds in doing this, he forces us to become dependent on everything except God for our daily spiritual, mental and emotional sustenance. Proverbs 14:12 tells us, "There is a way that seems right to a man, but its end is the way of death."

Remember, the enemy will always attempt to instigate a war in your mind to steer you away from the things of God and produce toxic dependencies in your life that become ties that bind your growth. God, however, wants you to know that the battle already has been won. All you need to do is believe and receive it as a decree for your life. Your spiritual growth depends solely on the Lord, His guidance and wisdom—as you acknowledge Him in all things.

Growing up under the welfare system, I witnessed firsthand the dependency that develops from relying solely on government assistance to feed a family and manage a household. This same dependency spilled over into my adulthood as I began to feel that people should automatically give to me and accommodate me whenever I needed help.

The power of God eventually broke this way of thinking as I learned that man should not live by bread alone but by every word that comes from the mouth of God. (See Matthew 4:4.) When we look to God, He will show us how to take care of ourselves.

Life as I know it today is void of any dependence on mankind. Instead, I depend totally upon God for my livelihood and my well-being. But this isn't the case for millions of people—including many born-again members of Christ's church.

The prayer my family prayed during our hard times and seasons of oppression was, "Lord, give us this day our daily bread." (See Matthew 6:11.) As we applied faith with this prayer, the dependency and oppressive spirit that had been hovering over us eventually began to lift. Yes, we were taken care of, but we were still oppressed. We were downtrodden and miserable until Jesus gave us a lift.

IDENTIFYING THE THIEF

Generally speaking, oppression can be defined as "a heavy, weary feeling of the body or mind." Spiritually speaking, oppression is a demonic spirit. When burdens seem too much to bear, fear can set in as a masquerading defense, setting you up for a total shutdown. Those who succumb to this emotional ploy are totally unaware of fear's masquerade, and they are further lured into the deceptive clutches of Satan.

> *The enemy will always attempt*
> *to instigate a war in your mind*
> *to steer you away from the things*
> *of God and produce toxic dependencies*
> *in your life that become ties*
> *that bind your growth.*

Oppression comes in many different forms and can enter through a variety of means. Nonetheless, one thing is consistent: Anytime the spirit of oppression is in operation, a universally acknowledged heaviness will attach itself physically and spiritually to the one being oppressed. This spirit will also present a struggle between the will of God and the will of man, and it will try to pull the person down, ultimately to death.

Anyone who has received Christ as Lord and loves God wholeheartedly yet still can't let go of that *one thing* that holds him captive to sin is struggling with oppression. As his born-again human spirit and fallen sinful flesh engage in battle, the body becomes fatigued and sluggish, causing further bewilderment within the mind. At this stage of the battle, the believer must make a decision to either buffet the flesh and surrender to the will of God or become so perplexed by Satan's lies that he gives up.

Unfortunately, many times the oppressed Christian decides within himself that he can no longer function under the heaviness of the oppression. So rather than continue fighting what the enemy has convinced him is a losing battle, he gives up and surrenders to the sinful drives of the flesh.

Oppression can originate in early childhood and can become a major factor in the shaping of a child's identity. If a child is constantly discouraged, belittled, embarrassed and humiliated by words of discouragement, his life can be framed within these barriers. The child then grows up to be an adult with low self-esteem and emotional dependencies. He struggles to succeed because the lingering spirit of oppression controls his life and keeps him down.

Frustrated, overly sensitive, jealous and competitive, the oppressed adult is incapable of handling constructive criticism. He reaches after his goals and ambitions as he trudges through one disappointment after another. Unable to face the risk of another letdown, he gives up again and again. Instead of allowing God to steer his life in the right direction, he allows life to control him and weigh him down.

This isn't a pretty picture, but sadly, you probably know someone like this. You may even be like this yourself.

DEPRESSION—
OPPRESSION'S KILLING PARTNER

Depression is one of the major side effects of the spirit of oppression. Depression causes gloominess and what many call "low spirits." This condition destroys the mind, clouds the thinking and further oppresses the individual who is already consumed by his burdensome state.

Like oppression, depression is no respecter of persons. It crosses gender, race and every social line and class. According to the Medical College of Wisconsin, some of the warning signs of depression are:

- Sleep disturbances—inability to sleep, sleeping too much or irregular sleep patterns
- Appetite disturbance—eating far more or less than usual
- Social withdrawal—refusal to go out
- Blaming yourself for your problems—feelings of worthlessness
- Inability to concentrate—even on routine tasks
- Thoughts about suicide[1]

Every one of these warnings indicates a tearing down of the body and mind. The enemy knows that if he can afflict the body by robbing it of food and sleep, after a while it will collapse.

But even more dangerous than these physical signs are Satan's devious, subtle ways of initially severing all contact and communication with loved ones and friends. Within this oppressing strategy lies his ability to secretly creep into the door as the only source of information. Here is where he deceives and disrupts the mind, eliminating those who care for you so he may have free rein. Satan then becomes the authoritative figure in his victim's life. I believe this may be why many times women seem to be more susceptible to the spirit of depression than men.

Women are by nature communicators. So when a woman's communication is cut off from friends and loved ones, the enemy immediately makes it his business to inhabit the newfound void in her life. And he does it through corrupt communication. This devious form of communication can be mentally implanted through subconscious thinking or ungodly counsel.

Women who are not involved in social or religious activities outside of the home can be more susceptible to oppression. It has been found that women who have structured themselves in multiple roles experience less depression than those who focus their lives in one area.

For instance, a single mother trapped within the welfare system who sits home all day watching soap operas and talk shows becomes major prey for the spirit of oppression. The enemy speaks to her mind through his fallen TV shows, causing her to give up and become depressed. Perhaps this is because the welfare system itself is a curse and carries with it a spirit of depression.

Think about it: Its name and all it stands for came from the greatest depression of them all—the Great Depression of the 1930s. So although the word *welfare* means "the state of well-being and prosperity," it still has not survived the curse attached to its name because of the false sense of security brought on by the welfare system. It has been said that one of the reasons the Great Depression bankrupted America was because the wealth at that time had been unequally distributed. That caused the stock market to become highly exaggerated, only to eventually crash, leaving the economy in a disaster. October 29, 1929, marked not only a great decline in the economy but also in the hope and self-esteem of American society as people were forced off their jobs with no means of support for their families. This day was known as "Black Tuesday."

Herbert Hoover was president at that time, and though he tried to keep hope in the hearts of the poor, people realized his words were empty. He had no proof to back them up. Franklin Delano Roosevelt defeated Hoover soundly at the polls at the close of his first term. Roosevelt's "New Deal" government work programs were then quickly implemented to help America out of those bleak days.

Years later, President Lyndon Johnson appeared on the scene, declaring a "War on Poverty" with such programs as welfare AFDC (Aid to Families with Dependent Children), food stamps and Medicaid. But without the proper structure and supervision, these programs proved to be a curse to many families. Some families have gone through generations depending solely on welfare as a means of support.

I say this not only because I personally grew up under the welfare system, but also because there are numerous children who are actually birthed into oppression through welfare and government-reliance. They become adults with the oppressive behavior and dependencies previously mentioned. The curse of low self-esteem and the spirit of criticism are oppressing millions within the welfare system.

Without a relationship with God or divine intervention, the welfare dependent's desire to better himself eventually dies. He finally gives up because flesh warring against flesh and flesh warring against the Spirit will eventually wear the body out and tear down the mind.

Welfare dependency is committed to making those who are bound by it a part of a permanent underclass. Because it is a curse, the system of welfare not only affects people financially, but it also affects them emotionally and is very degrading.

Yet the illusion says, "Don't be embarrassed—hold your head up. You deserve this. And besides, if you don't get it, someone else will." The enemy then continues the lies by telling them they can't get a job because no one is hiring, furthering the length of their impoverishment.

Welfare also separates the family, putting asunder the greatest institution on earth—marriage. The Bible says, "Therefore what God has joined together, let not man separate" (Matt. 19:6). But welfare says if there is a man (a husband) in the home, you can't receive assistance. This rule encourages "shacking up" and lying to stay afloat. God says marriage is honorable in the sight of the Lord, yet in the welfare system marriage is discouraged, and couples are penalized without warning. This unreasonable policy makes no room for an individual to gradually be weaned from the system to avoid economic ruin. The weapons of God's warfare are needed in this devilish fight.

> For the weapons of our warfare are not carnal but
> mighty in God for pulling down strongholds.
> —2 Corinthians 10:4

So even though welfare has proven to be helpful, this is normally the exception instead of the rule. Many people take what was meant to be a temporary means of support and turn it into a lifetime survival strategy. As a result, the spirit of oppression is left hovering over generations of children who grow up lacking any initiative to do better.

God's hand is always out to provide what you need, but you must reach up—not out.

No matter how long you may have been held captive by the spirit of oppression, you are never too young or too old to be set free. One touch from God can free you from a multitude of curses.

The Word of God sets men free when it is received as food for life and vision.

> Blessed is the man
> Who walks not in the counsel of the ungodly,
> Nor stands in the path of sinners,
> Nor sits in the seat of the scornful;
> But his delight is in the law of the LORD,
> And in His law he meditates day and night.
> —PSALM 1:1–2

In the pages that follow, I will attempt not only to enlighten but also to break this vicious cycle of oppression so that you will have God's power for victorious living. Remember, God's delivering power must be received with responsible faith. He offers no government freebies. His hand is always out to provide what you need, but you must reach up—not out.

FREE AT LAST

Blessed is he whose help is the God of Jacob,
    whose hope is in the LORD his God,
the Maker of heaven and earth,
    the sea, and everything in them—
    the LORD, who remains faithful forever.
He upholds the cause of the oppressed
    and gives food to the hungry.
The LORD sets prisoners free.
               —PSALM 146:5–7, NIV

Oppression knows no boundaries. It permeates the welfare system I grew up under, producing thousands of hopeless lives, and it stalks the business and educational communities because misery and failure know no social boundaries. And, yes, it stalks the church in an effort to cripple born-again believers with heaviness and fear.

Wherever this spirit can find a foothold, it will work to confuse, distract and cut off its victim from outside contact. Then it will fill that void with more deception to control clear-thinking minds. Sow an unchecked oppressive thought, and it will reap depression. When depression sets in, it will reap a harvest of sinful defeat.

Growing up in the church, I found out how a person can presume to be free while falling prey to the tormenting spirit of oppression. It happens without people even realizing what is taking place. This spirit isn't always as overt as one may think. In many instances, certain emotions can be so suppressed that the person being oppressed may never realize the reality of their state. Childhood or traumatic adult experiences are sometimes responsible for oppression's delusion.

There are some instances, however, in which an oppressed individual is very knowledgeable of their state, but they cannot imagine how God could ever set them free from something that has been part of their lives for so many years. Nevertheless, God knows exactly what area to touch and at what particular time to bring forth deliverance.

THE "A" WORD

One of the experiences that can form oppression within is sexual abuse. It happened to me when I was twelve. At a time when I was totally oblivious to the full extent of sexuality, a woman of experience took it upon herself to teach me about sex. For two long years, I was repeatedly called upon to engage in sexual acts with this woman that a boy my age should not have known about. To her it meant nothing, but it later caused me some temporary problems.

I bring this up to say I'm convinced that because of the oppression I endured from this woman, the door was opened later in my life to more perversion, whoredom and lawlessness. These were all oppressive spirits that came not only to strip me of my dignity, but also to destroy my character. I had convinced myself that time had healed me of these incidences. But I eventually found out that they had only been suppressed and that the spirit of oppression had packaged them neatly, only to open them later as a means of escape.

By the time I was a teenager, I had already been introduced to drugs and had developed a $270-per-day cocaine habit. To support this habit, I did whatever I was "bold" enough to do—snatching purses, robbing, stealing—all to satisfy my habit and hide within my secret place of escape. It eventually took a sentence in Rikers Island Prison for God to finally get my attention.

> *An honest relationship with yourself and Christ is your most beneficial commodity.*

Today, I no longer seek unreasonable approval of others. I am free to allow God to speak instead. Then, without questioning my own abilities, I obey. Now I know that it is not me who does the work, but Christ who lives within me. I can now walk free of the spirit of inferiority and low self-esteem. I freely preach, proclaiming that God is indeed real and that He will perform His Word until the end. God knew what area to touch at what particular time in order to bring forth deliverance in my life.

Yes, I had been saved and cleansed by Jesus' blood, and for years I'd grown and flourished in His grace and the call on my life. But there was a hidden enemy within my mind that had been suppressed, and it had been very active in my decision-making processes. It makes me wonder, *How many Christians today are still being steered away from God's best?* If you are one of these believers, don't be ashamed. Realize that an honest relationship with yourself and Christ is your most beneficial commodity. Denial is the door standing between you and your future. Freedom awaits you. All you need do is open the door and allow the healing process to begin.

> For everyone who asks receives, and he who seeks finds, and to him who knocks it will be opened.
> —MATTHEW 7:8

May God himself, the God of peace, sanctify you through and through. May your whole spirit, soul and body be kept blameless at the coming of our Lord Jesus Christ.

———

—1 THESSALONIANS 5:23, NIV

Nine

It's Your Move

God has sanctified us as a body of believers through one sacrifice—His Son Jesus. Upon doing so, He made an everlasting covenant with us that our hearts of stone could be turned to flesh and our minds renewed in Christ.

> I will give them an undivided heart and put a new spirit in them; I will remove from them their heart of stone and give them a heart of flesh. Then they will follow my decrees and be careful to keep my laws. They will be my people, and I will be their God.
>
> —Ezekiel 11:19–20, NIV

God has already prepared the way; all you need is the courage to obey His statutes. Jesus knows that the way has already been made; it was through His sacrifice that

Satan was defeated. This is why saints of God can find comfort in the fact that although the weapon may form, it does not have to prosper. (See Isaiah 54:17.) The battle has already been won. God never has to sit back scratching His head, trying to figure out how to deliver you from your next dilemma. He is Alpha and Omega, the beginning and the ultimate end, so before any battle is even fought the war is already won.

We are no longer captives to sin because the prison doors have been opened. All we need to do is step outside the confines of bondage and into freedom. Christ's redemptive power goes far beyond the physical boundaries, but unlike mankind who often works on the outward appearance first, God's transformation power is from the inside out. Unlike some of the traditional means of churches, who tend to strip everything that pertains to worldly pleasures (such as jewelry or certain attire), God is divine and knows that without a converted heart the appearance of discipline on the outside makes a person hypocritical and counterproductive.

> ### *God has already prepared the way; all you need is the courage to obey His statutes.*

The work you do—supposedly for Him—is in vain when the wrong motives are attached. Christ showed His displeasure of this way of thinking when He rebuked the scribes and Pharisees in Matthew 23:27–28:

> Woe to you, scribes and Pharisees, hypocrites! For you are like whitewashed tombs which indeed

appear beautiful outwardly, but inside are full of
dead men's bones and all uncleanness. Even so
you also outwardly appear righteous to men, but
inside you are full of hypocrisy and lawlessness.

It does not matter how "holy" a person might look
outwardly if on the inside he is full of rage, envy, strife,
jealousy, greed or whatever spirit may be driving him
away from God's plan. Those who allow Satan to hold
them captive in rebellion against God's Word are no
longer under God's authority, but instead they are
residing in Satan's domain. Satan is a leader of those
who are in rebellion and are disobedient toward God.

In which you once walked according to the
course of this world, according to the prince of
the power of the air, *the spirit who now works in
the sons of disobedience.*
—EPHESIANS 2:2, EMPHASIS ADDED

Because we often desire the best of both worlds, we
lack commitment to God and try to profess salvation
while holding on to the things of the world and lusts of
the flesh. But it is impossible to serve God and Satan,
for in trying to do so we displease God.

No one can serve two masters; for either he will
hate the one and love the other, or else he will be
loyal to the one and despise the other. You
cannot serve God and mammon.
—MATTHEW 6:24

Here we see one of God's most dynamic qualities at
work. Although He is all-powerful, He gave man a free

will; He will not force Himself upon anyone. When your appointed time for salvation has taken place, it is up to you to decide whom you will serve. We all do things that displease God from time to time, and even sin during our walk of salvation. However, we are not to wallow in our shortcomings; we must be quick to repent *and go and sin no more.* Because we were born with a sinful nature, a process is required to have this nature replaced with the nature of God. In the meantime, we are to experience and display victory while here on earth, not spend our entire lives waiting to die in order to experience the peace of God.

A person whose favorite testimony is, "It will all be over after a while," is usually a person who is not experiencing the benefits of peace, love and joy while here on earth. Just as it was never God's intention for us to live a terrible life of sin, it was also never His intention for us to live a "woe-is-me" life of salvation.

> ## *God gave man a free will; He will not force Himself upon anyone.*

In God's presence there is fullness of joy, and at His right hand there are pleasures forevermore. (See Psalm 16:11.) We are to be a walking, living witness so others can see the joy of the Lord, which is our strength, and the pleasures of knowing that He is our guide. Many times, however, we fall into the trap of believing that we are bound by Satan's cunning. Thus we become weary in our well doing, when in fact Satan has already been defeated. All we need to do is resist his traps, pray and be wise to his devices. We must realize that we must counter the enemy's violent attempts to take what God has given us with our own violent determination to protect the blessings of God that are present in our life.

SURVIVAL OF THE FITTEST

It's warfare, survival of the fittest, and only the strong will survive. But the strength I refer to is not physical but spiritual. The Bible declares:

> Likewise the Spirit also helps in our weaknesses. For we do not know what we should pray for as we ought, but the Spirit Himself makes intercession for us with groanings which cannot be uttered.
>
> —ROMANS 8:26

We are not to become complacent in our walk with God, but God wants us to realize the power we have within.

> ... having wiped out the handwriting of requirements that was against us, which was contrary to us. And He has taken it out of the way, having nailed it to the cross. Having disarmed principalities and powers, He made a public spectacle of them, triumphing over them in it.
>
> —COLOSSIANS 2:14–15

Not only did God take Satan's accusations against us with Him to the cross, but also He did it triumphantly, making a public spectacle of the principalities and powers of the enemy. Because of this, we don't have to experience any more guilt or condemnation. The sins of old are under the blood. God does not condemn. It is Satan who bears the weight of guilt upon us even after we are saved. God only convicts when we are in error, but He does not condemn. Condemnation says, "You're nothing; you can never be a true Christian, and your error proves that you never do anything right." Conviction says, "You must be careful not to be ensnared again into the yokes of bondage. What you did was wrong, but don't lie in your sin. Repent, and sin no more. You are forgiven." Therefore, you should never give anyone the power to condemn you or write you off because of wrongdoing. (See Colossians 2:16.)

Relationship with God is personal. The devil would have you believe that his power is greater than the power that dwells inside of you. This is because Satan desires to have your worship and your attention. The same worship that caused him to be thrown out of heaven in the first place is the same worship that he ultimately desires from us today. You must be wise to the devices of the enemy, whose main weapons are intimidation, manipulation and domination. Satan's strategy is force and trickery, but Jesus said, "But I, when I am lifted up from the earth, will draw all men to myself" (John 12:32, NIV). In other words, God does not have to use force, trickery or gimmicks to draw men and women unto Him; His Word does that all by itself.

The writer to the Hebrews tells us that "the Word of God is living and powerful, and sharper than any two-edged sword" (Heb. 4:12). Because it discerns the things of the heart, the Word of God has power to cut through the deceptive spirits of Satan and draw the soul of man from eternal darkness and lead him to God's eternal light.

So even when we pray, we are to put God in remembrance of His Word. It is the Word of God that pierces through darkness and reaches God, who releases what we need and sends it back to earth in the form of an answered prayer. The Word of God together with a sincere heart gets God's attention. You don't have to pray vain words of great literary quality to get God's attention; simply pray from your heart and release your faith.

> *God does not have to use force,*
> *trickery or gimmicks to draw men*
> *and women unto him; His Word*
> *does that all by itself.*

In Daniel 10:1–3, God had revealed to Daniel a vision. Upon understanding the vision, Daniel went into mourning, fasting and praying for three full weeks. In verses 5–6, Daniel was approached by a man "dressed in linen, with a belt of the finest gold around his waist. His body was like chrysolite, his face like lightning, his eyes like flaming torches, his arms and legs like the gleam of burnished bronze, and his voice like the sound of a multitude" (NIV).

Needless to say, Daniel was without a doubt in the midst of a divine visitation and about to finally receive a word from the Lord concerning his requests. Notice that in verse 12, the first thing that this man did was comfort Daniel. He assured him that although it may have seemed as if it had taken three weeks for his prayer to be acknowledged, God actually heard him on the first day he prayed and sent an angel with his answer. In verse 13 he explained his reason for the delay: "But the prince of the kingdom of Persia withstood me twenty-one days; and behold, Michael, one of the chief princes, came to help me, for I had been left alone there with the kings of Persia."

Finally, in verse 14 he explained to Daniel the reason for his coming: "Now I have come to make you understand what will happen to your people in the latter days, for the vision refers to many days yet to come." In this we see that persistence and patience prevailed in Daniel's circumstance. God immediately sent an answer to his prayer, but there was a demonic force that fought with the messenger to keep Daniel from receiving what he needed. This goes to show that even though God gives us the answers we need, we still don't always receive them. Because some of us lack patience and get angry too quickly when circumstances don't seem to go our way and in our timing, we revoke our own blessings. The prayer is answered, but we must continue to pray that the demonic strongholds that are hindering us from receiving our answer be destroyed.

There are no great mysteries for praying to God or destroying demonic strongholds. We need simply to invoke the power of God that resides on the inside of us, have faith and, most of all, not be intimidated by Satan's threats. The apostle Paul wrote, "God has not given us a spirit of fear, but of power and of love and of a sound mind" (2 Tim. 1:7). When we receive into our spirits the divine revelation of the gift God gave us when Jesus died on the cross, we will then realize just how much clout we have with God.

NO LONGER CAPTIVES

Because of this clout and His power living within us, we are no longer captives to the law of sin and death. "For what the law could not do in that it was weak through the flesh, God did by sending His own Son in the likeness of sinful flesh, on account of sin: He condemned sin in the flesh" (Rom. 8:3). This prevents Satan's fear tactics from having victory over the saints of God. We know that we have victory over Satan and sin because clearly they both have already been condemned. The thing that holds most of us captive and stagnated, however, is our desire for comfort at almost any cost.

I once ministered to a young woman about bad decision-making and the price she was willing to pay for temporal happiness. As it turned out, because of her troublesome past, she had begun to do a number of things that were totally out of character for her in order to enjoy life to its fullest. She said she had missed out on several opportunities because she spent too much time building and perfecting the dreams of others, so now she wanted to do some things for herself—including dating a man with whom she had fallen in love with, who just happened to be married.

This man was everything she had missed yet always desired: loving, caring, concerned for her needs. He was independent and strong-minded, yet very sensitive to her every need and desire. And most of all, to her amazement, the love she felt toward him was reciprocated. He cared for her emotionally, financially and physically. It seemed as if they were one; before she could even voice her need, he was right there to fill the void. In ministering to this young woman, I posed a simple question to her: "What price are you willing to pay for a temporal escape, no matter how good it seems? You have to determine within yourself just how much you're worth and if you're priced too low. Jesus already paid for you. So why are you selling yourself out again when *the* Man Himself, Jesus, already considers you so invaluable that the only way He could show you was through His death?"

It was then that she began to realize that though this man seemed to give her the happiness and fulfillment she desired, she was again being tricked by the illusions of Satan. She began to see the real picture as she found herself again putting her life on hold—waiting for his calls, rearranging her schedule to spend time with him, literally waiting at his beck and call. Her life revolved around this man, who was another woman's husband. She had become so free in her thinking that she had returned again into bondage, and until that moment she had not even realized it.

Don't Return to Bondage

One of the most cunning tactics of Satan is to deceive us into becoming so free in our religious rituals, beliefs and way of thinking that we return to the bondage from which we have been delivered. Paul wrote to the Corinthians, "Be careful, however, that the exercise of your freedom does not become a stumbling block to the weak" (1 Cor. 8:9, NIV).

This is true today as well. When you have confessed Jesus as Lord, you can no longer hide beneath the umbrella of "what I do is my own business." This motto can no longer be your guide when what is done places your life and the lives of others in jeopardy. The Bible declares that we who are strong should bear the infirmities of the weak and not just be concerned about pleasing ourselves. (See Romans 15:1.) Just as a child watches his parents and patterns his behavior after them, many times those who are newly converted look to the older saints as examples of godly living.

No parent who is accused of neglecting or endangering a child can go before the judge with the excuse, "Well, they should have known how to take care of themselves instead of looking to me for guidance." By all counts, this person would be pronounced "guilty as charged." Likewise, we who are more mature in Christ must take into account the fact that those who are new creatures in Christ may not be as knowledgeable about the things of God. Therefore, we must often be living epistles of the life of Christ. And yes, we all must "work out [our] own salvation," as Paul wrote in Philippians 2:12. However, those who because of their negligence and reckless endangerment cause a child of God to stumble and fall away from the faith shall be pronounced "guilty as charged" when we stand before our Judge. Jesus told His disciples in Luke 17:1–2, "It is impossible that no offenses should come, but woe to him through whom they do come! It would be better for him if a millstone were hung around his neck, and he were thrown into the sea, than that he should offend one of these little ones."

NO LONGER IGNORANT

We no longer have to be ignorant concerning the mind of God. The devil's greatest means of attack is giving us the appearance of victory, then suddenly snatching the curtain to reveal our bondage. But we no longer have to be ignorant of his devices. Jesus came to set the captives free. So it is no longer we who are in bondage, but Satan. He has known this for quite some time, yet he gives us the illusion that servitude to him is much more pleasurable than servitude to God. Once again he has been exposed. His authority is limited only to those who willingly embrace his ideologies. But even in situations of cooperative bondage, God knows how to say, "Enough is enough," and bring deliverance to our loved ones if we just continue to pray, remain steadfast and increase our faith.

God is all-powerful. He knows what we need and when we need it. God's Word is the only truth that cannot and will not fail. "It is easier for heaven and earth to pass away than for one tittle of the law to fail" (Luke 16:17). It's your move, your moment, your time. Move forward into the abundant blessings of your God-given inheritance.

There is therefore now no condemnation to those who are in Christ Jesus, who do not walk according to the flesh, but according to the Spirit. For the law of the Spirit of life in Christ Jesus has made me free from the law of sin and death.

—ROMANS 8:1–2

Ten

It's a New Day

Now that the devices of the enemy have been exposed in your life, you can lay your religion down and feel no guilt about it. Religion is a term used loosely to acknowledge belief in some type of higher power. It offers a method of worship, sets boundaries and shapes a person's beliefs and world-view. Rarely is religion backed by facts or power; it often hinges on the conjured beliefs of those who have been introduced to "a god" of tradition, but unfortunately they usually fail to see the awesomeness of the risen and loving Savior. Religion often presents God as some type of ogre waiting to punish those who disobey His command or fall away from His statutes. He reminds us, however, that "My grace is sufficient for you, for My strength is made perfect in weakness" (2 Cor. 12:9).

By faith we are able to recover and remain in the

divine will of God during very trying times. Sometimes while in the hands of others—people who are supposedly there to uplift and assist us in our growth—we are negligently mishandled. Too often they come close to dropping us spiritually, nearly causing us to abort our spiritual destiny because of their negligent behavior. If we are ever to have victory here on earth, we must learn and understand the promises our heavenly Father made to us. That way we can no longer be conned or intimidated by the devil. The blessings of the Lord are at our fingertips daily, but tragically many of us fail to realize just how continually accessible are God's answers to our needs and desires. There are no tricks, gimmicks or hidden tactics for provoking the blessings of God. Simply *ask in faith,* and you shall receive.

In Mark 11:22–24, Jesus admonished the disciples:

> Have faith in God. For assuredly, I say to you, whoever says to this mountain, "Be removed and be cast into the sea," and does not doubt in his heart, but believes that those things he says will be done, he will have whatever he says. Therefore I say to you, whatever things you ask when you pray, believe that you receive them, and you will have them.

DIVINE ORCHESTRATION

We must understand that much of what we go through is to build character in us and is by the divine orchestration of God. In 2 Samuel, we see an extraordinary relationship between David and Jonathan, two young men from different lifestyles, yet as close or closer than blood brothers. Neither of them knew, of course, who would die first, but because of the covenant they had with each other, they knew that one would take care of the other's seed. So in 2 Samuel 9:1, we see that because David outlived Jonathan, he asked of the household of Saul: "Is there still anyone who is left of the house of Saul, that I may show him kindness for Jonathan's sake?" Here we see the word *kindness,* which is where the word *kindred* or *family* is derived. Family is normally the beacon of any community. It is within our families that we come together, discuss life's circumstances and resolve conflicts. Jesus employed a similar principle when He sat with the disciples, sharing with them parables and the truths of God.

> ## There are no tricks, gimmicks or hidden tactics for provoking the blessings of God.

David showed kindness to Mephibosheth, Jonathan's son, by allowing him to eat with him at the king's table. Mephibosheth was Jonathan's crippled son that few knew about. He had been dropped by his caretaker as an infant, causing him to become lame. Since it was not good for the royal family to have anyone with visible handicaps, Mephibosheth had been tucked away, hidden, his identity kept secret from others. "So David said to him, 'Do not fear, for I will surely show you kindness for Jonathan your father's sake, and will restore to you all the land of Saul your grandfather; and you shall eat bread at my table continually'" (2 Sam. 9:7).

We all know of the decor at a king's table. It's covered with lace and is finely draped with purple and gold cloth covering the entire table, leaving only an inch between the floor and the drape. It's indeed a table "fit for a king." This means that when Mephibosheth was placed at the table, no one was able to see his crippled frame. No one could tell that he couldn't walk. This is a very significant point. Many of us today unknowingly uncover our weaknesses to others. Yes, many of us have been dropped and left as cripples or maybe even left for dead. God may never change the fact that we were dropped, abused, raped or used, but He will alter the assignment of Satan so that when we sit down at His table, the fine linen of Christ our King will cover us and keep us in His divine care.

All God wants you to do is sit down at His table while He covers your hurts, pain and weaknesses and releases your deliverance and healing from the super-natural realm into the natural. God just wants you to dine with Him while He supplies your every need. In areas where you feel you can't walk, talk or whatever the case may be, God will appoint someone to do those things for you. He will do whatever it takes to ensure that you receive from Him your inheritance and have everything restored that the enemy has stolen.

If we as the people of God would simply grasp the significant principle of dining with the King, many could break free of weaknesses left behind after past traumatic experiences. We must learn to "[forget] those things which are behind and [reach] forward to those things which are ahead" in order to reach "the goal for the prize of the upward call of God" (Phil. 3:14). God knows our every need and how to supply it at the time we need it most.

A Clear Understanding of Faith

Not only did our Father promise to supply all our *needs,* but He also promised that whatever we *desire,* we can have (Phil. 4:19; Mark 11:24). There is only one stipulation: We must pray in faith and not waiver. In order to increase and release our faith, we must first have a clear understanding of the definition of faith. Literally speaking, *faith* is having complete *trust.* But the Bible goes further; it says, "Faith is the substance of things hoped for, the evidence of things not seen" (Heb. 11:1). This means that in order to completely trust in God, we must believe that what He has promised has already been done, though we may not physically see the things we desire, and that those requests will be made manifest in the natural.

God will do whatever
it takes to ensure that you receive from
Him your inheritance.

Jesus tells us that when we pray according to His will, if we *believe* that we receive, we will have whatever we ask in faith. For many of us, it's hard to believe that this is all it takes to receive from the Lord. This is because our natural minds will not allow us to believe that all we need to do is just ask for something and have it granted to us. Most of us are used to receiving what we ask only when we pay for it. So it is hard to believe that not only did someone else already pay the price for us, but also He is willing to give to us whatever we desire.

Some might even ask, "Now why would God do

that?" The answer is that God is not a man. He doesn't think the way we think, nor does He give to us based upon our good behavior.

As parents, we reward our children for good grades in school, appropriate behavior and so on. But God does not just give to us based upon our goodness or righteousness. The prophet Isaiah wrote that our righteousness is as filthy rags (Isa. 64:6). It's by the grace of God that He blesses us, even in spite of ourselves. This is not to advocate bad behavior, but in all honesty, we can all recall a time that, in spite of our iniquities, God looked beyond our faults and saw our need. Many times He has blessed us *really good,* when in fact we were *very bad.*

God has dealt to us all a measure of faith (Rom. 12:3). Therefore, you should never allow anyone to deceive you into thinking that you don't have faith. The problem may simply be that your faith has not yet been activated. For instance, when you receive a credit card in the mail, no matter how valuable the card may be, it is of no use until you call the number listed on the card to have it activated. The same principle applies to faith. We have all been given the measure of faith we need. However, it is up to us to have this faith activated to receive from God the things we need and desire.

How do we activate this faith? "Faith comes by hearing, and hearing by the word of God" (Rom. 10:17). Studying and hearing the Word of God on a consistent basis can activate your faith. Many of us, because we come out of very dogmatic and legalistic church doctrines, find it very hard to believe the God we serve could bless us in spite of our imperfections. This does not give us the license to sin, but it simply lets us know that God is faithful and merciful, and He does not revoke His plan so easily from our lives.

Never allow anyone to deceive you into thinking that you don't have faith.

Because we as saints of God are sometimes very uninformed, we forfeit God's plan by listening to Satan's lies. A person who is uninformed and finds himself again indulging in ungodly territory may find it very difficult or impossible to find his way back to God. This is because he has been taught that when his gift has been offered up to the world instead of God, the Lord will no longer honor that gift. Thus, he convinces himself that God and the anointing have left him; therefore, he would have more success by offering this gift to the world rather than "bothering" God by trying to repent and get back on track. This is condemnation and a great deception that the saints of God have allowed Lucifer to pour into their minds for quite some time.

The writer to the Hebrews wrote, "For He Himself has said, 'I will never leave you nor forsake you'" (Heb. 13:5). We are the ones who leave Him through ignorance and the bad teachings of religion. The apostle Paul wrote, "For the gifts and the calling of God are irrevocable" (Rom. 11:29). God is merciful despite our lack of knowledge and unbelief. The only way we can truly know God's character, however, is to get to know Him on a personal and intimate basis, and the only way to accomplish this is to spend time with God in prayer and Bible study.

Just as Peter, by faith, walked on the water in Matthew 14:29, our daily walk with God is by faith and not by what we see. It was by faith that I received the calling of God on my life to preach His Word with boldness, despite those who do not even believe in the God I preach about. And certainly the background from which I came did not, under any circumstances, assist me in accepting this call. However, I was often told that *no one* from my family would ever amount to anything—a message sent straight from the pits of hell. So upon receiving this message as truth, much of my life was spent fulfilling, not the plan of God, but my lawless desires of drug addiction, rebellion and gambling with death. But by the grace of God and His divine mercy, God still did not revoke His blessings over my life.

Even when I—as Peter did in Matthew 14:30—again lost faith and began to sink, all I had to do was cry out to the Lord, "Save me!" Immediately Jesus stretched forth His hands and caught me. (See Matthew 14:31.) From that point until the present, God has given me the faith and favor I need not to lose faith when the boisterous winds begin to blow. Throughout our Christian walk there will continue to be trials, tests and temptations, but the good news is that we have been equipped with the proper weaponry to engage in battle against doubt and unbelief. For many years, the kingdom of God has suffered against the violent tactics of the enemy, but if we are to receive what already belongs to us and what was left to us as an inheritance, then we must be just as violent. (See Matthew 11:12.)

SEE YOURSELF
AS GOD SEES YOU

In 2 Samuel 9:8, Mephibosheth, one who had given up the fight, inquired of David, "What is your servant, that you should look upon such a dead dog as I?" One of the first things God has to do is to change your opinion of yourself. This is because when you see yourself as God sees you, it gives you a brand-new determination and a brand-new state of mind. Allowing God to give you self-esteem enables you to trust totally in Him and to know that He loves you enough to meet your needs and desires. Mephibosheth was looking at David's present state as king and ruler of many. *Certainly,* Mephibosheth must have thought, *King David could not possibly want me—a nobody—to dine with him.*

Mephibosheth was reared in Lo Debar, "a place of no pasture." After being in this environment for a number of years and listening to the negative comments of others, he began to receive their opinions and believed he would never amount to anything. He may have thought God had overlooked him. But actually, though the people may have failed to see him as the intelligent person he was because of his physical disability, God was always there. Mephibosheth had been judged for a long time by his outward appearance; all he needed was the opportunity just to sit at the king's table and be heard. It was at the king's table that he realized he was just as good as those around him.

Perhaps you have had a Mephibosheth experience. The good news is that you don't have to faint under the pressure. Instead, keep your focus; don't miss out on the blessings of God when He invites you to the King's table. Paul wrote, "And let us not grow weary while doing good, for in due season we shall reap if we do not lose heart" (Gal. 6:9). Acknowledge this as an opportunity to leave the past behind, and arise in a prosperous and exciting new day.

You may have noticed that while reading this book, the Lord began to open your eyes and reveal the true essence of your surroundings. Perhaps every time you picked up the book to read it, you found yourself distracted—the phone rang, there was a knock at the door, the children started fighting. The devil will do whatever it takes to stand between you and your deliverance. But this marks a new day, a new beginning. In order to maintain your deliverance, you must embrace your freedom as a lifestyle.

Allowing God to give you self-esteem enables you to trust totally in Him.

Jesus reminded the disciples in Matthew 17 of the importance of prayer and fasting as a lifestyle in order to combat the forces of the enemy. A man had brought his son to the disciples to cast the devil out of him, but the disciples could not. So they inquired of Jesus, "Why could we not cast it out?" (v. 19).

Jesus answered:

> Because of your unbelief; for assuredly, I say to you, if you have faith as a mustard seed, you will say to this mountain, "Move from here to there,"

and it will move; and nothing will be impossible for you. However, this kind does not go out except by prayer and fasting.

—MATTHEW 17:20–21

First, notice that Jesus stressed the importance of faith accompanied by action. He didn't mean that we should apply faith, fasting and prayer only when confronted by the devil, but that we must apply it to our spiritual walk continually. Had the disciples been praying and fasting as a lifestyle, they would have had the faith to set this young man free.

Next, check out your spiritual and physical surroundings. Be honest about what has been your greatest hindrance, and lay it before the Lord in prayer. You might be surprised at some of the things the Lord will reveal to you when you submit to His will and acknowledge Him as Lord over every area of your life. You may be required to make a physical change in order to rid yourself of some accursed things that have held you back and prevented the voice of God from directing your life.

Now the LORD had said to Abram: "Get out of your country, from your family and from your father's house, to a land that I will show you."

—GENESIS 12:1

Before Abraham could see the land of God, he had to leave the familiar land of his family. Whatever the case may be, remember to seek God continually, throw off what holds you back, and find true relationship with the Father. As I agree with you in prayer, release your faith and know that victory belongs to you on this day and forevermore.

Father,

I agree in prayer with Your child that every stronghold is now broken in the name of Jesus. I bind every religious spirit that has hindered him or her from receiving Your Word and knowing who he or she is in Christ Jesus. You said in Your Word that whatever I bind on earth shall be bound in heaven, and whatever I loose on earth shall be loosed in heaven. So I bind every inferiority complex in the name of Jesus. I bind every oppressive force that has ever plagued the life of the individual reading this book, and I loose the blessings of God in the name of Jesus.

Now, God, I pray that every seed of righteousness that has been planted will take root and not be plucked by the devices of Satan. I come against every stronghold, and I thank You for the victory and for the testimonies that will come forth from the person to whom You're speaking to right now. In Jesus' name, amen!

Notes

CHAPTER 2
DELIVERANCE FROM TRASHY TRADITIONS

1. Stephanie Nolen, "Birth Over, Nigerian Teen Awaits Flogging," *Toronto Globe & Mail* (December 28, 2000). Retrieved from the Internet on June 26, 2003 at www.commondreams.org/headlines/122800–02.htm.

CHAPTER 7
CANCEROUS SEX

1. "Tracking the Hidden Epidemics: Trends in STDs in the United States, 2000," Centers for Disease Control. Retrieved from the Internet July 24, 2003 at www.cdc.gov/nchstp/dstd/Stats_Trends/Trends 2000.pdf.
2. "Syphilis," HiTOPS.org – Syphilis. Retrieved from the Internet on July 1, 2003 at www.hitops.org/health-clinic/syphilis.shtml.
3. Ibid.

CHAPTER 8
OPPRESSION—LOOSING THE TIE THAT BINDS

1. "Signs of Depression," *HealthLink,* Medical College of Wisconsin. Retrieved from the Internet July 25, 2003 at http://healthlink.mcw.edu/article/901291354.html.

OTHER PRODUCTS
BY BISHOP GEORGE BLOOMER

BOOKS

The Little Boy in Me

Witchcraft in the Pews

When Loving You Is Wrong, but I Want to Be Right

101 Questions Women Ask About Relationships

The Battle Plan

Crazy House, Sane House:
When Your Marriage Drives You Crazy

This Is War—Engaging in Spiritual Warfare

Weapons for Warriors

Empowered From Above

Authority Abusers

VIDEOS

You Dropped Me, God Caught Me

I'm Not Who I Told You I Was

It's Mess That Makes You

Man in the Mirror

Now How Are You Going to Get Home?

The Tomb Is Empty

Warning, Angels in Charge

It's the Law

Mining Your Mind

Let's Go to the Other Side

What's in the Bag?
Cockroaches & Bootleg Preachers
Witchcraft in the Pews
Crossing Over
Look Who I'm With Now
Where Eagles Fly
Hem of His Garment

SERMONS ON CD

Apples & Oranges

10 Stupid Things Women Do to Mess Up Their Lives

STDs
(Sexually Transmitted Deceptions and Spirits)

I Had a Dream

Order...Order...Order

When God Reveals Himself

Now That the Raven Has Gone

CD SERIES

Anointed for an Appointed Time

To order or to obtain more information,
call or contact:
G. G. BLOOMER MINISTRIES
515 Dowd Street, Suite 204
Durham, NC 27701
(919) 688-1476

No sugary, sweet words to just make you feel good...

Your eternal life is at stake, and Bishop George Bloomer has words you need to hear! We pray that you have found encouragement and fresh spiritual insight within the pages of *Throw Off What Holds You Back*.

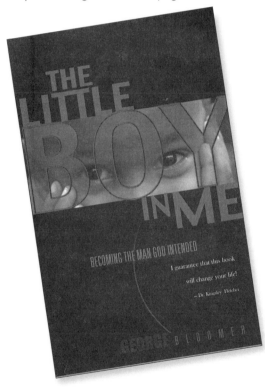

Bishop Bloomer has also written a book for men (and the women who love them) that will change how you look at God, yourself, your wife, your kids and your future.

"Within this text are the keys for men held captive by the little boy syndrome and for the women who must deal with them. The Little Boy in Me is a powerful book that will add value to your life."

—Pastor Kirbyjon Caldwell,
Author of The Gospel of Good Success
*Windsor Village United Methodist Church,
Houston, Texas*

$12.99 / 0-88419-75Q-6

Dispel the deception in your life today!